HISTORY OF RESISTANCE

TU Senan

History of Resistance
written by TU Senan

Second edition: September 2013
First edition: December 2012

Classification: TU Senan
history/politics/economics/sociology

ISBN 9781870958585

A catalogue record for this book is available
from the British Library

Published by Socialist Publications

Printed by Russell Press Nottingham

Distribution by Tamil Solidarity
205 Well Street,
London E9 6QU

info@tamilsolidarity.org
www.TamilSolidarity.org

Cover photos:
Front: Workers at a general strike meeting in the auditorium in Colombo 28 July
1980
Back: Troops guard parliament buildings during the general strike and state of
emergency 08/08/1980
All photos courtesy of the Socialist

Edited by Hessie Sachs and Sarah Sachs-Eldridge

Thanks to Bob Labi, Keerthikan, Charles Anthony (London), Sathiyaseelan, Jon
Redford, Naomi Byron, Meena Kandasamy
and many others who gave valuable comments and corrections.

Introduction to second edition

This edition includes a number of corrections and clarifications. An introductory chapter, glossaries and maps have also been added.

In the short time since the initial publication some of this book's perspectives have been borne out, in particular by the advent of major student and youth protests in Tamil Nadu and in the diaspora. However, the history of struggle in Sri Lanka will also offer rich and valuable lessons to these movements and their leaders. To this end the chapter that deals with the events of late 1969 and the 1970s has been extended.

There is no claim that this book is an exhaustive history covering all aspects of the resistance in Sri Lanka. Much has been left out to keep the book precise. Our aim in producing it is to pick out and analyse the key events and processes which provide invaluable understanding for the necessary struggles today and in the future.

September 2013

Map of Sri Lanka

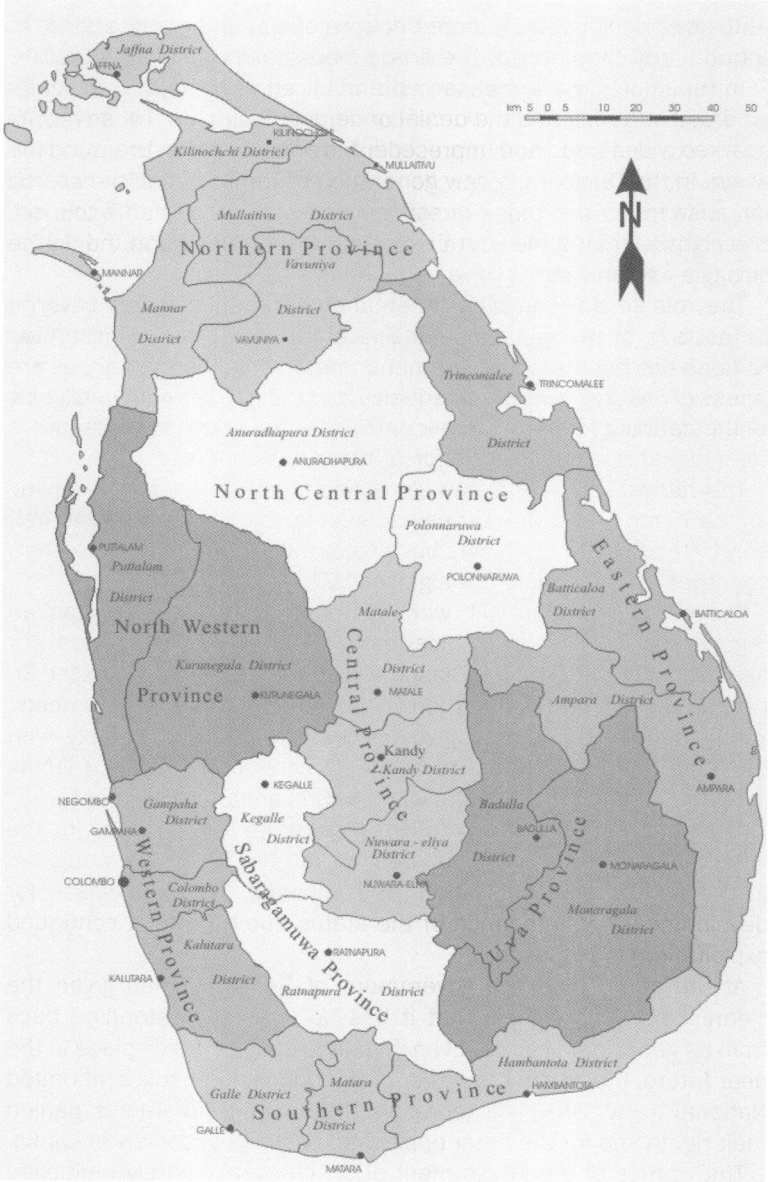

Introduction to first edition

At the end of May 2009, three decades of war in Sri Lanka came to a brutal and bloody end. The final phase saw as many as 100,000 Tamil-speaking people massacred, and the survivors faced with state-enforced suffering and the denial of democratic rights. These events sparked widespread and unprecedented anti-war protests around the world. In the Diaspora, a new generation of Tamils began the search for answers to the many questions posed by what had occurred. Since then, among the youth especially, the issues surrounding the struggle for Tamil rights have been increasingly debated.

The role of the so-called 'international community', its inaction in the face of genocidal slaughter and the hypocrisy of the United Nations and of western governments are here deliberated on, as are issues of wider geopolitics, inequality and the fundamental problems of the capitalist system. Developments within these spheres give a clear signal that the struggle for Tamil rights is not over.

The radicalisation of a new generation, angry over the trampling on the rights of the Tamil-speaking people, is seen as a threat - not only by the Sri Lankan regime but also by the governments of western countries in which there are significant Tamil populations.

The new generation will, without doubt, engage the Sri Lankan regime and its allies in political battle. A massive propaganda war against politicisation in the Diaspora is already being waged by the Sri Lankan regime, and by institutions sponsored by other governments. Young people are told to give up the struggle and comply with the 'safe' (and failed) tactics of the Tamil National Alliance (TNA), including seeking to negotiate with the Sri Lankan government.

Attempts are being made to regenerate confidence in the 'international community' as well as in the Sri Lankan regime. In the name of 'reconciliation' and 'in order to create space for development', maintenance of the status quo (in effect, continued exploitation) is proposed.

At the same time the government of Sri Lanka has given the clearest possible signals that it has no interest in stepping back from its genocidal policies. Even if 'regime change' takes place in the near future, the coming to power of the opposition neoliberal United National Party (UNP) will represent little change for Tamils denied their rights and for the other oppressed sections of society in Lanka.

The worries of the government of Sri Lanka are surely multiplied when they witness the radicalisation of young people in Tamil

Nadu, India, alongside the processes taking place in the Diaspora. These developments represent the building of the first base of a new struggle. That means that we must expand and intensify our political understanding and master the economic and social laws that determine social, political and economic relationships.

The Tamil Solidarity campaign has produced this book because it believes that a clear understanding of history is a vital tool and guide in the struggle for our rights. We study the lessons from movements of the past to strengthen the movements of today, but we do not live in the past.

There is no shortage of books written on Sri Lankan history. The majority, however, are popular works which are either tainted by the author's own sense of national identity or written almost as text books serving the interests of the state. A number of books do not even mention the 1953 general strike – a key event in Sri Lankan history. They do this to undermine the role of united struggle at key turning points in history, as their views are restricted by nationalism. Similarly a number of books claim that Sri Lankan independence was 'granted' by the British - not won.

Sinhala nationalism has been whipped up by various mythology – so-called 'historical' accounts of kings and kingdoms. Ancient religious texts are used as scientific proofs. Tamil nationalists, also drawing on false folklore, present alternative accounts, accounts which serve only the likes of the TNA in its attempt to maintain political control over Tamils. Neither faction appears to have learnt the lessons from history and nor does either show a way forward beyond attempting to carve out niches for themselves.

The truth is far from simple. We – those who want to strengthen the fightback – have nothing to gain from either version of history. We must examine the history in detail and, in particular, the history of struggle.

Historical events are never random events – there are always contending forces that determine social activities and historical processes. The history of any society is a history of struggle between oppressive forces and those who fight back. Whether it is the fight among the kingdoms or during colonial times or after independence, the people's rights are never granted by their oppressors. Our history is not the history of kings and queens – instead it is a rich history of development and culture and resistance against oppressive forces.

This book borrows heavily from various previous works. It tries to bring together the key points to provide a full grasp of the development of the national question in Sri Lanka. The link between the labour movement activities and nationalism (used as a tool to counter workers' struggle) cannot be ignored.

The intention is also to reveal the main forces that drive historical events: how two contending forces, the oppressed masses (poor workers and peasants) and the exploiting class (elite, capitalists, etc) struggle for their own interests. Which force wins at each stage is determined by various factors, including, in particular, the existence of a leadership with a clear programme.

The details and lessons of a history of Sri Lanka can, not only help us avoid repeating mistakes, but aid us in devising a strategy, tactics, and above all, a programme for bringing power to the majority – the oppressed masses. Only by doing so can we hope to abolish the injustices and inequalities that exist.

This small book is planned as an aid to discussions. Tamil Solidarity welcomes feedback. Please point out any omissions which can be included in future editions.

The land and its people

Sri Lanka, known as Ceylon during colonial times and known as Lanka or Eelam before that, is a small island situated in the Indian Ocean just to the south east of India. Human existence on this island is dated back to the Palaeolithic period.

Over time the island has had various names; it was called 'Serendip' by Arabs. From the early 16th century Portuguese and later British invaders contributed to its pre-independence name, Ceylon. Immigration and migration have featured in the history of this island.

Given the proximity, the relationship with India was a dominant factor. Whenever empires or big kingdoms in India expanded into the Indian Ocean, various groups of people settled in Lanka and mixed with the existing population.

It is generally agreed that the island was first unified under one administration under British rule. Prior to the colonial period various kingdoms and other independent feudal territories existed. Over time a few key power centres emerged, among them Jaffna in the north, Kotte in the south and Kandy in the central Hill Country. Historically Tamils lived in the north part of Sri Lanka and are often associated with the Jaffna kingdom.

However this period, over thousands of years, is only very partially recorded, as is the case in every part of the world. It is widely believed that the tiny number of remaining Veddas (hunters) could be the original inhabitants of the island. Today the island is also home to Sinhala, Tamils, Muslims and many other minority groups, such as Burghers (European Sri Lankans), and Malays (east Asian Sri Lankans) and others.

The Sinhalese majority population speak the Sinhala language and are mainly Buddhist. Some argue that the Sinhalese are descendants of Vijaya, the son of King Ashoka who came from West Bengal in around 550 BCE. This claim is made in early Buddhist literature.

Although the island was invaded by various empires that emerged in south Asia, historians have not yet pinpointed which kingdom was responsible for, or the exact period of, the origins of the Sinhala language. But it is generally believed that the use of Sinhala language could date back thousands of years. Sinhala is unique to the island and is classified in the Indo-Aryan language group, which also includes Bengali, Punjabi, Gujarati and many more.

There is no reliable survey available regarding population size.

However, among the total population of 21 million inhabitants around 75% is believed to be native Sinhala-speakers. They are concentrated mainly in the southern and western parts of Lanka. Of course, the Sinhala population itself is far from homogenous. The Sinhalese living in the Hill Country area, in the middle of the island, used to differentiate themselves from the southern Sinhalese. Such differences among the Sinhalese, including caste differences, have receded, in part due to economic development. Buddhist religious practice had an impact on weakening the caste divisions.

The Tamil-speaking people in Lanka comprise three main groups, although, of course, there are further divisions inside each section of the population, which we will address later.

Tamils, who mostly live in the north and east part of the island, have lived in Lanka for thousands of years. Some believe that the Veddas and Sri Lankan Tamils were the same family and the original inhabitants of the island.

Those who dispute this theory date the arrival of Tamils on the island to around the tenth century CE – during the time when the Tamil kingdoms developed in South Asia. However, respected historians believe that the history of Tamils on the island dates back thousands of years.

Tamils in Sri Lanka differ from the Tamils who live in Tamil Nadu, a large south Indian state. The Tamil language is shared but is spoken in a distinctly different way and there exist many cultural differences.

Tamils in Lanka are estimated to make up around 12% of the island's population, which reflects a shrinkage caused by the war among other reasons. The majority of Tamil-speakers are Hindus.

The majority of the Muslim population in Lanka speaks Tamil. They are called Moors by some historians. They are considered to be descendants of the Arab traders who travelled to Sri Lanka from around the eighth century CE. They live in the north and east, although they are mainly concentrated in the east part of Sri Lanka. Their population was reduced in the north following mass expulsion during the war. Due to this major aggression as well as the historical oppression and exploitation they suffered at the hands of both Sinhala and Tamil leaders, they identify as separate from the other Tamils living on the island. Muslims are estimated to make up around 10% of the population.

Tamils living in the Hill Country areas have traditionally been isolated, socially and geographically, from the other sections of the Tamil-speaking population. Colonial exploiters in the 19th and 20th centuries brought them to the island from Tamil Nadu, India to work in the tea plantations. They constitute around 5% of the population after forced mass extradition to India by the Sri Lankan state in 1964 depleted their number. Sinhalese people lived in and around the Hill Country areas before and after the arrival of Indian Tamils. The British colonials used the resulting linguistic and cultural segregation to keep this vital workforce in impoverished conditions and to fuel the national differences, to their advantage.

The question of which ethnic community has the 'rightful ownership' of the island is a major source of friction given the ethnic tensions that emerged since independence from British rule.

Tamil nationalists say that three kingdoms existed before British imperialism - and the north and east are their country and homeland.

Sinhala nationalists say that Tamils were recent invaders from India and the whole island belongs to the Sinhalese. Both cite various research and documents to support their arguments, most of which are disputed and questionable.

While there is a heated debate about who are the so-called 'indigenous' people, no one disputes that both Tamils and Sinhalese have been living on the island for hundreds of years – probably more than 2,000 years.

So Tamils have a clear claim to the part of the land where they have lived historically. Who came to the island 'first' is not the key question. The Indian Tamils, who are the relatively recent immigrants to Sri Lanka, have lived in the Hill Country for centuries and have a rightful ownership to that land.

However, the Sinhala Buddhist-dominated state has consistently disputed Tamil rights in an attempt to establish its own authority among the Sinhala masses. The current regime is even trying to alter the demography of the north and east to further the long-established divide and rule tactics.

Origin of Kandyan Buddhist sentiment against Tamils

The growth of Buddhism is linked to the resistance against the rigid caste system in India, later challenged by the Hindu revival. Tamil and Sinhala Buddhists were burnt alive in their thousands. Buddhist stupas were destroyed and Hindu temples built on their sites. This mass persecution played a role in fomenting the Buddhist antagonism against the Hindu Tamil kings.

Kandy, located in central Sri Lanka, is a beautiful hill area and a centre of Buddhism. One of the most sacred temples for Buddhists, the Dalada Maligawa or the Temple of the Sacred Tooth Relic, is located in Kandy. In 1815, after more than 70 years of rule by the Nayakkar, a king of Telugu Tamil origin, a rebellion by the Buddhist Kandyan court provided the background for anti-Tamil sentiment in the Kandyan court.

Between 1796 and 1800, anger against the grinding tax system imposed by the British government, gave rise to anti-British rebellion across the country. The rebellion was supported by the Kandyan Kingdom which sent resources and army personnel to the north as well as to the south. In 1803, the British government's attempt to capture Kandy suffered a major defeat. But the British managed to split the Buddhist monks in the Kandyan court, a number of whom began to conspire against the Kingdom. The last King of Kandy, who was said to be particularly brutal, accused one of the best known monks of treason and had him and his family publicly killed.

This event sharpened the division between the monks and the Kingdom. The monks responded with a massive propaganda campaign. Two sections of their religious literature (Kirala Sadesaya and Vadiga Hatana), produced at the time, provide examples of how anti-Tamil ideas developed. They describe how a 'Tamil King' failed to respect the Buddhist court. Next, the narrative is directed against the Tamil people as a whole. The description of Tamils in this literature resembles the description of Hindu priests.

The British colonisers seized this opportunity to help the Kandyan court to overthrow the Nayakkar dynasty. In order to maintain control, the British signed a covenant in 1815 in which the cruelties and oppression suffered under the Tamil king are referred to. The covenant also proclaims: "that all claim and title of the Tamil race to govern the land of the Sinhalese people is abolished and extinguished". However, the covenant was never implemented and failure to do so led to widespread rebellion against British rule between 1817 and 1818. But in 1818, after the ruthless suppression of another rebellion, the colonisers took control of the Kandyan Kingdom and, with that, full control of the whole of Ceylon which previous colonial rulers had never managed to do.

Arrival of the Tamil plantation workers

The Slave Trade Act for the abolition of slavery in the British Empire was passed in 1807 and was implemented by 1808. But the slave trade and slavery itself were only finally abolished in Britain in 1833 by workers' action and the continued uprising and resistance of blacks held captive in the British colonies. Abolition changed the way British rulers acquired and transferred labour in the colonies. To maximise their profits they employed and exploited local and imported workforces as cheaply as possible.

In India, caste division provided the ideal opportunity for exploitation. The caste system, preserved by the continuation of feudal relations in the subcontinent, provided bonded labour that was more or less the equivalent of slave labour.

In Sri Lanka, Kandyan antagonism towards the Tamil-speaking people assisted the imperialists' exploitation of the workforce. Indian Tamil plantation workers were transported to Sinhala-dominated areas, far away from the traditional Tamil homelands of the north and east. The upper caste Tamils of the north refused to identify with the poor oppressed caste plantation workers. These were factors which gave major advantages to the colonialists to exploit their imported tea workers to the full, and the plantation economy flourished.

As early as 1818 the then British governor, brought thousands of labourers from south India to solve the labour shortage which followed the Kandyan rebellion. The first batch of workers arrived in 1923. The majority of these workers were from the poorest and most oppressed castes in India.

Demand for reform and privileges

In order to facilitate the export and transfer of labour and commodities, British imperialism developed an infrastructure in Sri Lanka. The immense size of the empire forced British rulers to employ small groups of 'assistants' to control the colonies on their behalf. Its reliance on local populations to control and manage labour and other resources increased as infrastructures to facilitate the transportation of commodities were developed. In turn, reliance on local 'assistants' led to the growth of a small English-speaking elite drawn from the upper caste and the families of the wealthy landlords who, in turn, were made more wealthy by taking a small share of the colonial exploitation.

Similar to the 'mulattoes', the wealthy mixed race, in Saint-Domingue who, at the end of 1879, appealed to the Constituent Assembly in France to be treated as equals of white people, the wealthy class in Sri Lanka demanded constitutional reforms to accommodate their interest. The development of the tea plantations in the later part of the 19th and early 20th century led to the emergence of affluent groups in Sri Lanka, similar to those in the Caribbean who had flourished due to the cultivation of sugar and other export commodities.

In 1885, to obtain these privileges, high caste individuals founded the Indian National Congress. This party, formed as a 'Hindu Party', swore loyalty to the throne but demanded a greater share in government for 'educated Indians' – mostly, members of the upper caste. In 1919, the Ceylon National Congress was formed. The Congress was composed of high caste/class individuals who had no interest in genuine independence for the country or, for that matter, any matters outside of their own privileges.

Religious backlash against missionaries

Privileged families wanted to send their children (sons mainly) to the schools to which the 'white rulers' sent their children. Many privileged children attended schools run by missionaries while others, to further their studies, were sent to England where they stayed with priests and their families. These children underwent a strict Christian education.

On returning to Ceylon, many rediscovered their families' traditional religions. Using the Christian missionaries' preaching techniques, they confronted white Christian hegemony. What began as religious revival by educated youths took on an anti-colonial character and won mass support.

The Hindu reform movements that originated in India, led by Sri Aurobindo, Dayananda Saraswati and others, as a reaction against the offensive propaganda of Christian missionaries, acquired an anti-colonial aspect. Not infrequently, members of the reform movements used the language, the tactics and some of the brutality that the Christian missionaries used. Sri Aurobindo had been to St Paul's school in London and had won a scholarship to Kings College at Cambridge University. He later became the leader of the Indian nationalist group, seen as extremists for their readiness to use violence and who advocated outright independence.

In Sri Lanka, in the south, Buddhist nationalism was led by Anagarika Dharmapala. In the north Hindu nationalism was revived by Arumuga Navalar. Both, like Aurobindo in India, had undergone a strict Christian schooling.

Riots led by religious leaders

Religious national movements mobilised the masses in a way which the English-educated 'moderate' elite never could. Mass meetings were held. In their fight to get greater political representation, the local capitalists, themselves unable to mobilise the masses, took the side of the growing religious movements. However, they did not support these movements completely.

In the late 19th century the local merchant population was dominated by Muslim traders and the Nattukottai Chettiars (traders, merchant-bankers and moneylenders). In 1880, in the Colombo suburb of Pettah, trade was dominated by 86 Chetty and 64 Muslim firms with only a handful of Sinhalese traders among them. During this period, too, Dharmapala, the son of a rich furniture dealer from Pettah, directed an attack against the Muslims. In 1915 he wrote:

"The Muhammedans, an alien people… by Shylockian methods become prosperous like the Jews. The Sinhalese sons of the soil, whose ancestors for 2,358 years had shed rivers of blood to keep the country free from alien invaders… are in the eyes of the British only vagabonds…The alien south Indian Muhammedan comes to Ceylon, sees the neglected villager, without any experience in trade… and the result is that the Muhammedan thrives and the son of the soil goes to the wall."

March 1915 marked a century since the Kandyan convention. With the mobilisation of the rural poor based on Buddhist Sinhala ideology, anti-imperialist movements were building up and beginning to assume a national character. By the end of May, Buddhist riots against the 'Coast moors', the name given to Muslims who were recent immigrants from the Malabar coast in South India, caused a great deal of tension leading to violence. The violence spread and 35 Muslims were killed and 198 injured. Eighty-six mosques and 17 churches were damaged, and over 4,000 shops were looted.

With similar anger and unrest developing against them in northern India, the British rulers moved quickly to arrest the Buddhist leaders, including Anagarika Dharmapala's brother. The majority of the Muslims who were attacked spoke Tamil. Anagarika Dharmapala carefully selected 'Southern Mohammedans' for attack.

But the Sri Lankan Tamil elite that emerged, mainly from the upper caste, did not care about the Tamil-speaking Muslims who were coming under attack. In fact the Tamil elite of the time came to the defence of their Buddhist counterparts. Sir Ponnambalam Ramanathan, a leading right-wing Tamil politician, condemned the way the British suppressed the riots. While seen, on the one hand, to be mounting opposition to British imperialism, on the other, he alienated a wide layer of the Tamil-speaking Muslim population. Later, by defending the hard-core Sinhala nationalists he alienated the Tamil workers as well.

The Hindu ideology of the Tamil elite came from Arumugam Pillai (navalar) who declared that the 'three Ps' – parai (drum, it indicates in particular the drum used by the Dalit oppressed caste); pen (the woman); and the panchama (the Dalits, oppressed caste) – were all born to be beaten. Pillai vigorously opposed the admission of the oppressed castes and women into schools, etc. His Hindu revivalism also led to an increase in attacks on the oppressed castes.

A different direction in India and Sri Lanka

The inability of the religious leaders to lead a successful fightback against imperialist oppression led to the collapse of mass support for them. But in India Mahatma Gandhi rescued these leaders and brought them together in the Congress Party.

The British did not face the same situation in Lanka. In fact, the Sri Lankan elite were not capable of replicating what Gandhi was doing in India. However, some educated youths, inspired by the workers' movements, formed an organisation called the Lanka Youth League. This League was the first organisation with a political programme to be formed on the island. It brought together trade union activists, students and youth. The formation of this organisation in the south and, in 1924, of the Jaffna Students' Congress in the north, changed the course of the history of Sri Lanka, making it very different from that of India before and after independence.

Some students and other visitors from the colonies to Britain had been involved in the trade union movement and other anti-imperialist activities in Britain. They had observed the confidence of the British working class. However, unlike in Britain and other industrialised countries, the colonies did not have fully formed workers' or mass movements. Consequently, because the same conditions that applied in Britain did not apply in Ceylon where the local capitalist class was weak and played second fiddle to imperialist forces – they could not, on their return home, replicate the British institutions.

Elite divide - workers unite

To suppress the independence movement the governor of Ceylon, William Manning, reformed the legislative council and the first elections took place in 1921. That election resulted in 13 Sinhalese and three Tamils being elected to the legislative council. These results differed from those of the previous election in which each community was allotted one seat, an equal distribution. The Tamil elite campaigned for the restoration of equal representation. Manning, who, in order to establish a support base, had initially favoured the Kandyans, now saw the opportunity, using Tamil discontent, to sponsor division among the elite.

Before and during the period of World War One (1910-19), world trade fell. Despite the growth in rubber production and war industries, commodity prices plummeted and wages either stagnated or were reduced.

At that time a significant number of plantation and textile workers took to the streets to demand their rights in Sri Lanka. The strike wave that followed between 1919 and 1921 was a new phenomenon that brought together many sections of workers. The railway workers and Colombo harbour workers – a key workforce at the time – led several strikes. They demanded a wage increase and a reduction in working hours, etc.

A poll tax was introduced requiring every male in the country to pay two rupees or work on road construction for six days. AE Goonesinghe, leader of the Young Lanka League, organised a successful campaign against this poll tax leading to its abolition in 1922. In September of that year, following the poll tax victory, the Ceylon Labour Union was formed. The general strike which followed in 1923 saw the entry of the organised working class into politics.

Events in Sri Lanka were heavily influenced by what went on in Britain. The actions of the British working class were an inspiration to workers in the colonies. In Britain, after a hung parliament failed, the Labour Party came to power for the first time and formed the government. In 1926, British workers led the great General Strike. Despite its ultimate defeat the strike had a significant ripple effect in the colonies, sparking movements and inspiring resistance.

Who fought for independence?

The religious movement had shown that the masses wanted to fight back against their colonial oppressors. Because of their anti-colonial sentiment, the privileged sections of the community began to rely on the support of the masses.

In 1926 Sir Hugh Clifford, the British colonial administrator, announced that the island's constitution was inadequate and appointed a special commission, headed by the Earl of Donoughmore, to examine it.

The British agreed with the elite leaders of the Ceylon National Congress (CNC) that: "New measures should be designed to train the Ceylonese for eventual self-government." But the CNC's demands were largely reactionary. It opposed women's suffrage and demanded that, to be eligible for the vote, a man must earn at least 50 rupees a month, a large sum for that time. Its members discussed at length who could and who could not be trusted to use their vote 'sensibly'. They even admitted that their demands "might lead to the accusation that it [CNC] was seeking to establish an oligarchy". Incredibly, a section of the CNC, mainly the older leaders, argued that Sri Lanka was not ready for self-government!

Formidable opposition to the Donoughmore Commission came from young students in London who were active in the Ceylon Student Association (CSA). They participated in the conference of the League Against Imperialism organised by the British Communist Party. Several meetings and other activities against the Donoughmore Commission were held in London.

1929 was a remarkable year and the events that took place in it taught the members of the CSA a great many lessons, including bringing them the theory of 'permanent revolution', as proposed by one of the leaders of the Russian Revolution in 1917 that saw workers take power, Leon Trotsky. In 1930, before returning from

Britain, some of the members, such as Philip Gunewardena, tried to make contact with Trotskyist groups in Spain and France.

The Jaffna Youth League, influenced by the Indian National Congress (INC), boycotted the first election to the State Council, demanding immediate self-government. A group of seven British MPs had been sent to India in 1927 to study constitutional reform. The group was commonly referred to as the Simon Commission after its chairman, Sir John Simon. The Commission was widely opposed. INC youth members, calling themselves 'young socialists', initiated a boycott of the Commission.

Then came several prominent INC visits to Ceylon, almost all to Jaffna: Mahatma Gandhi in November 1927 and Jawaharlal Nehru in 1931. In a speech, Nehru, who was active in the young socialists within the Congress party, directed the youth towards radical action. He urged: "Freedom is worth striving for, but you must see how it affects the bottom dog in your country, and try to understand the nature of imperialism and capitalism".

Another prominent INC leader, Kamaladevi Chattopadhyay, who considered herself a feminist and socialist, also visited Jaffna and participated in organisational meetings. Her presence helped to bring together several youth leagues. In 1931 the youth leagues formed a Youth Congress headed by Aelian Pereira. The Congress immediately called for "downright unadulterated independence". Chattopadhyay spoke at the opening meeting of the Congress. Students, who had returned from London with socialist ideas, joined the youth congress.

Even though many political leaders, such as Nehru, called themselves socialist, they did not have a full understanding of socialism. Nevertheless, their minimal leaning towards the left gave rise to movements within the oppressed class and, significantly, within the oppressed caste.

The Tamil elite, who opposed the leftist youth leagues, used the caste system to reinforce its dominance. The majority of the youth leaders came from the upper caste.

1931 also saw violence against the oppressed caste in Changanai, a northern town. The dominant Vellalar caste members accused the oppressed Paraiyar caste of hiring 'drummers', a practice forbidden to them, and attacked them. Through this distracting and dividing tactic and similar methods the elite regained control.

The Tamil elite fought the electoral boycott and, in 1934, managed to hold another election for seats which had become vacant. The election resulted in the emergence of another layer of right-wing politicians. Among the newcomers were GG Ponnambalam, elected for the Point Pedro area, and SJV Chelvanayagam. K Balasingam and V Duraiswami, who participated in organising the boycott, did not stand for election.

Suriya Mal movement

The Suriya Mal movement, which was taken up by the Colombo Central Youth League, galvanised the country. Ceylon's contribution to the Poppy Fund for war veterans had been one of the largest in the British Empire. The anti-Poppy Day campaign spread quickly. Taken up by the young socialists of the Suriya Mal movement and with sales of another flower, the suriya (sun flower), Poppy Day took on a different character. The money collected was used for the education of children from deprived communities. The leaders behind the movement also argued against entry into the imperialist World War Two.

In 1933 workers at Wellawatte in Colombo, the largest textile mill in Ceylon, employing over 1,400 workers, went on strike against a reduction in wages. Their trade union, headed by AE Goonesinghe, proclaiming that the strike was illegal, refused to represent the workers and unleashed racist slanders. In response, socialist students, active in the Youth League, formed a new trade union and put up a spirited fight for the workers. This event and the other industrial action which followed, distanced Goonesinghe from the workers. His anti-Tamil, racist views were successfully countered by the workers' solidarity shown in the many industrial actions organised by young socialists.

A malaria epidemic in 1934 affected a great number of people. It is estimated that at least 125,000 people died. The Youth League organised a campaign to get food and medicine to the people. For their efforts, Philip Gunewardena, NM Perera, Colvin R de Silva, and many other students were revered by the suffering masses.

In 1935, following the support gained from the masses, leading members of the Jaffna Youth League and southern young socialists came together to form a new political party called the Lanka Sama Samaja Party (LSSP). Not only was the LSSP the first political party to be established, it was the first party to demand total independence from Britain. Founding members declared that the fundamental aim of the LSSP was to establish a socialist society. Notable was the fact that among the 40 founding members at the conference, a considerable number were Tamil socialists. As, at that time, no word for socialism existed either in Tamil or Sinhala, the name, Sama Samaja, was coined especially. However when the division between the Tamil and Sinhala masses sharpened, the name, which was a Sinhala name, was to prove to be a further barrier between them.

World War Two

The LSSP's opposition to World War Two quickly took centre stage. In fact, the opposition's stand was to play an important part in the history of Sri Lanka. In India, Gandhi, set out to defend the British Empire. He abandoned his Satyagraha (a philosophy and practice of non-violent resistance) and urged Indian men to fight for the British.

In contrast, the LSSP opposed the war. In his speech to the State Council on 28 August 1936, Philip Gunewardena declared: "Sir, we are not ready to fight the battle of the imperialists. We refuse to be cannon fodder for coining money for the dividend hunters of England."

The support built up during the Suriya Mal movement helped the LSSP members in their campaign against the imperialist war. In adopting this policy, the LSSP was also taking a stand against the Stalinists and the Third International. With the Soviet Union, by then a deformed version of the idea of a workers' state as envisaged by Trotsky, VI Lenin and their party the Bolsheviks, under attack from Germany, joining the Allies, the Third International urged workers everywhere to support the Alliance and so defend the 'workers' state'.

In contrast, Leon Trotsky opposed support for the war on the grounds that it was an imperialist war. The core of the LSSP, having read Trotsky's works and beginning to identify themselves as Trotskyists, denounced the Third International's call for support for the Allies.

Elites play divisive role

The Tamil and Sinhala elites fought each other for positions on the legislative council. GG Ponnampalam began to intensify his '50-50 representation' campaign in 1938. The campaign brought him popularity among the Tamils in the north where the Sinhala elite was increasingly discriminating against Tamils in general. In August, 1944, with the support he received for his Tamil nationalist views, Ponnampalam formed the All Ceylon Tamil Congress (ACTC). By the 1940s, when ministerial and other government positions were solely occupied by the Sinhala elite, a Tamil nationalist campaign was in full swing.

DS Senanayake, a leading member of the Ceylon National Congress, was particularly concerned about the growth of the left. One of the reasons given for his resignation from the CNC was the influence of 'communists' within it. In September 1946, Senanayake formed the United National Party (UNP). Until then, the Ceylon bourgeois had not had a party to represent them.

Independence?

Ceylon has great strategic importance. During the war the British, in order to safeguard their economic interests, gave in to the demands of DS Senanayake, their most conservative ally. Today, even right-wing historians believe that it was fear of the left that led to the official announcement on 18 June 1947 that the island would receive 'fully responsible status' within the British Commonwealth and that DS Senanayake's proposals would be adopted.

Initially the intention of the British had been to grant a new constitution by 1953. But to safeguard the interests of British imperialism power was transferred to the local bourgeoisie immediately. Granting of dominion status had become urgent as the means to stabilise a situation in which the left wing had begun to develop a mass base.

A series of strikes had taken place in 1946, including a strike of government workers. But the general strike of May-June 1947 was the most significant of all. It was then the largest strike to date. More than 50,000 workers in both the public and the private sectors participated.

The then governor of Ceylon, Sir Henry Monck-Mason Moore, later wrote: "I was in Kandy at the time and George E de Silva urged me to take immediate action. I went to Colombo and met the ministers, who all urged me to declare a state of emergency and exercise dictatorial powers. Somehow or other they had come to know of the existence of such an instrument, though it was highly secret.

"I then pointed out to them that they had full powers to pass

legislation of the same character in the State Council and that if they considered the time had come to take such action it was their plain duty and responsibility to take the necessary action themselves. If they did so I would of course support them in every possible way and they could base their legislation on the draft in my possession. Eventually they did so, and indeed provided more severe penalties than in the original draft in my possession. It was quite obviously an attempt to leave me holding the baby if such strong action was criticised."
(British Governors of Ceylon by HAJ Hulugalle, ANCL, Lake House, Colombo, 1983, p232)

The resolution to break the strike was quickly passed. The above quote summarises the attitude of both the colonialists and the local capitalist elite towards the workers' movement. One of the key things to note was the solidarity of the strikers. A Tamil worker, Velupillai Kandasamy, was shot and killed when the police brutally attacked a workers' demonstration of thousands headed by NM Perera. When Kandasamy's body was released, Sinhala and Tamil workers, followed by a massive procession, carried the body from the hospital to the Fort station. This demonstration of working class solidarity terrified the establishment. Even Solomon West Ridgeway Dias Bandaranaike, (later to become prime minister and one of the architects of the Sinhala-only language act), later remarked: "The shot that killed Kandasamy sounded the death knell of British imperialism!" The united struggle of the workers played a key role in pushing out British imperialism. Tamil trade union activists such as Bala Tampoe, K Vaikunthavasan, AR Asirwatham and Geoffrey Gunanayagam emerged from the strike.

Role of British imperialism

United struggle – particularly the united struggle of the workers, peasants and poor – played a key role in forcing the British rulers to give up some control over the island. At the same time a natural alliance was forged between the British rulers and the emergent local ruling elite. This elite was responsible later for the attack on the rights of workers, minorities and others. However their masters cannot be exempt from having responsibility for it. The British rulers' policy, the devastation it caused, and the deep divisions it created, should not be underestimated.

The British rulers promoted all possible divisions when it suited them. The British used the religious, ethnic and caste divisions to maintain their control. They set one section of the population against another. They consciously developed a loyal clique, repaid with privileges and power, to control the rest of the population. In order to do this they maintained many of the feudal relations that existed in the subcontinent, including the caste system.

Their ruthless exploitation caused famines and immense suffering. Every country occupied by the British empire is left with a huge scar. Those who fought back were able to mobilise the population regardless of the various different identities due to the common suffering as a result of British rule. This must be acknowledged.

Incredibly, there are some who argue that if the British maintained their rule Tamils would have benefited. Nothing can be further from the truth. It is true that so-called independence did not bring the results that the masses hoped for. However the continuation of British rule would have led to further suffering.

Capitalists fight to consolidate power

Although DS Senanayake managed to gain power for the capitalists and small business owners, he was still faced with the massive challenge of consolidating that power. His fears came true in the first election, held in August 1947, but the Tamil Congress leader, GG Ponnambalam came to his aid and joined his UNP government. Senanayake became the first prime minister of Ceylon. The LSSP came second, winning ten seats. In all, the left took 19 seats despite standing in only a limited number of constituencies

In the power-hungry politics that followed the elections, equality was thrown out the window. In 1949, a section of the Tamil Congress, led by SJV Chelvanayagam, broke away and formed the Federal Party, in Tamil called the Illankai Tamil Arasu Kachchi (ITAK – Sri Lanka Tamil state party). The Ceylon Indian Congress composed mainly of plantation workers did not join the UNP government. By not voting for the UNP, the plantation workers sent a clear signal to that Party.

Once in power, the first steps Senanayake took were to counter the 'threat' of the left. He immediately passed a number of repressive laws and launched an attack on the plantation workers' rights. The Parliamentary Election Act of 1949 denied plantation workers citizenship and the right to vote. As, in any case, the UNP did not have the support of the plantation workers, they lost nothing by passing this legislation. They hoped, however, to halt the plantation workers' growing support for the LSSP and reduce the representation of the Tamil-speaking people in that party. To win support for his actions, Senanayake used the age-old Kandyan antagonism against the Tamils. Sinhala Buddhist nationalism again began to take centre stage. The ruling elite hoped nationalist tensions would cut across the rapidly developing workers' movement and so secure their power base.

The Public Security Act of 1947 and the trade union act of 1948 were aimed directly at breaking the workers' parties and organisations. The Act and the encouragement of Sinhala Buddhist nationalism ensured that the UNP obtained a considerable majority in the next election. Tamil Congress leaders gave the UNP unconditional support in its attacks on the poor and the workers in the plantations and throughout the country.

It is not surprising that Tamil leaders such as Ponnambalam lost support among ordinary working class people - particularly the Sinhala working class - some of whom may have supported them in the past. The loss became clear in the next election when the Tamil Congress lost several seats. It was this loss that forced them later, in their attempt to hold their share of seats in parliament, to take up Tamil Hindu nationalism.

A section of the UNP split away, under SWRD Bandaranaike, fearing that the hard-line right-wing policies of their party might lose them the support of the rural Sinhala population. In 1952, Bandaranaike formed the Sri Lankan Freedom Party (SLFP) and, borrowing phraseology from the left, promised that his party would be 'the salvation of the poor'.

In the elections of that year, the SLFP won nine seats, equalling the LSSP vote. However, the elections were, in the main, a triumph for the UNP. In fact, with the Tamil plantation voters excluded, the UNP gained a massive victory, winning 54 seats. The UNP was now established as the party of the capitalist classes from all ethnic backgrounds – Tamil, Sinhala and Muslim. It relied largely on the capitalist and petit bourgeois classes. Tamil Congress suffered a loss, winning only four seats, while SJV Chelvanagam of the Federal Party lost his seat to UNP.

Boosted by their election victory, the UNP leaders convinced themselves that they had successfully defeated the workers' movement. They began implementing policies to benefit their class. During their first term in government, over 50% of the government money went on welfare and services. Economic downturn during the second term was accompanied by the beginning of an attack on public services. Food prices rocketed. The price of rice first doubled, then tripled, then went through the roof. The working class, having organised numerous strikes, including general strikes, in the past few years, needed to show its strength once more. Just one year after the election came the heroic 1953 general strike that shook the country.

Great general strike of 1953

During the 1950s the young finance minister JR Jayewardene (JRJ) and his pro-capitalist policies were very unpopular among workers. This finance minister, later to become prime minister and president, stands out in the history of Sri Lanka, as the single biggest threat to civil liberties (present ruling Rjapaksa dynasty excluded) and the architect of the major crisis and civil war in the country.

Jayewardene was a known right-winger, notorious for his hatred of the left. Time and again in parliament, the LSSP leaders quarrelled with him for interrupting their speeches with sarcastic comments or personal attacks. He was the first right-wing UNP leader to rely on thugs in order to make political gains. He implemented right-wing policies with no regard for the workers and the poor.

With the help of the American economist, John Exter, Jayewardene was behind the establishment of the Central Bank of Ceylon. Exter, who became the Bank's first governor, worked closely with western economists, including those from the US and Australia. Jayewardene was also instrumental in allowing the then McCarthyite US government to use Colombo airport for military purposes. For him 'reds' posed a major obstacle. He used all measures to get his way and had all the characteristics of a dictator. He forged close ties with the United States and other western imperialist countries and implemented western friendly capitalist policies.

As finance minister, Jayewardene was largely responsible for plunging the country into economic chaos. In 1952, soon after the UNP's victory, he cut the farmers' subsidy. Food rations were reduced and prices rose. The rice price hit the workers and the poor particularly hard. With an increase in imported goods, foreign reserves soon dried up.

The Korean War began in 1950. The US intervened and, for a while, the Sri Lankan economy boomed. As the Cold War intensified, Trincomalee Harbour, on the east coast in the Tamil-speaking area, about 110 miles northeast of Kandy, became increasingly significant. With India taking the Soviet side in the Cold War, the US needed a reliable base in South Asia. The US placed an embargo on some imports from Ceylon and urged it to cut its ties with China, which was offering considerably more money for Ceylon exports than was the west.

The British Governor (still in power at that time) and Commonwealth officials put pressure on loyal UNP members to take a hard line against the left. The Cold War had already begun to have an impact in Ceylon. Despite the advantages of links with China, the UNP government decided to import from the west which meant the country had to pay more for imports. In the hands of Jayewardene, the economy collapsed like, in the words of a Tamil proverb, 'a garland in the hands of a monkey'. It was absolute madness, at that stage, to cut subsidies and provide incentives to the private sector. Whereas, earlier, Jayewardene had declared that: "Ceylon's financial position was sounder than it has been ever before", within one year his economic policies had brought the country's financial system to its knees. The LSSP, aware of the workers' anger over these policies, called for action.

Workers had already begun to take spontaneous action. On 20 July 1953, over 5,000 people attended a Jaffna meeting against the removal of the rice subsidy. The meeting lasted five hours. The next day, over 12,000 port workers went on strike in Colombo. Wellawatte spinning workers and, on the 23rd, weaving mill workers staged a half-day's strike. In Kankesanturai 8,760 people signed a petition calling on their MP, S Natesan, to vote against the budget. Meetings were held in Kandy, Jaffna, Kopay, Ruwanwella and elsewhere all around the country. At each meeting LSSP members spoke and council workers and trade unionists participated with thousands of workers attending. At each meeting a resolution was passed pledging support for a strike - known as the Hartal- which was scheduled for 6 August.

The pro-capitalist or capitalist-owned media attacked the 'reds'. They pointed out that 6 August "coincided with the meeting in Moscow of the Supreme Presidium of the Soviet Union, at which the Dictator of the Soviet Union was expected to announce a change in Soviet policy." On 26 July 1953 Jayewardene, by means of Radio

Ceylon, warned strikers that: "public servants who keep away from work as a protest against government policy or to force government to change its decision on any matter will be considered to have vacated office and such officers will not be reinstated." However, despite his diatribe against the 'reds' and threats to workers, the strike plans went ahead rapidly. Jayewardene began to blame Tamils for 'taking a bigger share of the economy', etc. Capitalist historians and politicians have often called him a clever man! But as far as the workers were concerned, he understood nothing about society. In 1953, their views were proved to be correct.

The clique which had suppressed the 1947 general strike was once again in power. It decided that if the strike took place, the army would be called in to take over the harbour and help the police to forcefully drive the workers back to work.

While accepting Jayewardene's financial blunder, R Premadasa, another UNP leader who later became prime minister in 1977, accused the "leftists of trying to exploit the situation." Incredibly he asked the people to "accustom themselves to leading a simple and inexpensive life." In the run up to the strike day he declared: "I make bold to predict on this occasion that this hartal will be best joke for this year. I make bold to tell those reds, make no mistake, people will come and listen to you but they will not believe an iota of what you say."

His wishful thinking never became fact. People came to the meeting. They came in their thousands. They listened and they took action. After a delay due to disagreement between some trade unions controlled by the Communist Party, the general strike was called for 12 August.

The whole country was brought to a standstill. The solidarity and strength of the strike surprised even the LSSP leaders. Military drivers were unable to break the transport and port workers' strike. Such concerted action by the workers had never been seen before nor was it to be seen again. Bala Tampoe, the general secretary of the Ceylon Mercantile, Industrial and General Workers' Union (CMU) and a Tamil member of the LSSP wrote that the strike: "taught both the workers and the rural poor that, together, they are fully capable of challenging and even smashing the forces of the capitalist state. Never again will the police force hold any terror of them, when they have decided to meet it in direct struggle. The day of 12 August 1953 will be remembered as the day when hardly a policeman was seen in Maharagama, Boralesgamuwa, and other places... the masses now know that the police and military, together even, are too few to withstand them, when they are ready to die, as did more than one hartal hero."

But the media reports of the strike were pure fairy tales! The Ceylon Daily News reported that "work goes on today". The editorial was entitled "Business as usual" and gave detailed accounts of how life was 'very normal' on the day of strike. On that 'normal' day, the UNP government's cabinet met on board the HMS Newfoundland, a British warship in Colombo harbour. The next day, the panic-stricken government declared a state of emergency and issued curfew orders for the southern and western provinces. The same media that reported that the great people of Ceylon had ignored the strike and that business was 'as usual' began to explain 'what the emergency means'. Despite the state of emergency and the curfew, the following days' papers were full of news of workers' actions around the country. By 15 August the army had to move in to take control of the cities. On 19 August the same Ceylon Daily News, quoting the London Times, wrote: "knowing well how to exploit a grievance they [the workers] were successful in organising a general strike on an impressive scale."

On 1 September 1953, the LSSP MP Robert Gunewardena expressed the workers' anger in the parliament: "This government acts upon the advice given to it, by the American embassy to the finance minister. You are aware, Mr Speaker, that the government sent out an urgent message and got down 20,000 rupees worth of armaments. Yes they are descending once more to their traditional habits! They are selling out this country to American Imperialists. It seems to me that the descendants of that family who once sold the country to the British imperialist, that family of traitors, that family of the finance minister, are now ready to betray this country to American imperialism. If this is so, how is it possible for us to have any faith in the government?" He was interrupted by the Speaker and the UNP members and forced to sit down after calling for a vote of no confidence.

GG Ponnampalam and his contemporaries in the Tamil Congress, along with the Tamil elite and big business friends, supported the UNP and JR Jayewardene's policies. They deplored the strike and argued vigorously against the demands of the thousands of Tamil workers. During the strike the Tamil elite had shown their loyalty to the UNP and clearly demonstrated which class they belonged to and where their interests lay.

On 12 October 1953 Prime Minister Dudley Senanayake was

forced to resign. Despite his attempts to threaten members of parliament physically and excusing his own inaction on the grounds of ill health, he was no longer capable of winning victories for the capitalists. John Kotelawala became Ceylon's third prime minister.

Having sacrificed the prime minister, the UNP made concessions to the strikers in order to consolidate its ruling position. The capitalists feared they had lost the battle to the left. To boost its morale, the international capitalist class came to their aid. In 1954, the British queen visited Ceylon. She celebrated her 28th birthday there. Despite all the help and fanfare, it took 20 years for the UNP to recover. Due, in part, to the betrayal by the leaders of the LSSP, recovery came at the workers' expense.

SWRD Bandaranaike, who did not support the strike, came forward to express communal sentiments. However, at this stage he was careful not to anger the workers, as he had to rely on some LSSP support in parliament and he feared that the workers would come back to punish him as they did the UNP.

The LSSP failed to fully recognise the power of the workers and what they required. Even though the LSSP had led a heroic struggle, its leaders were unable to convert the struggle into one of winning power for the working masses. Later this mistake limited their ability to provide independent leadership to the working class, and eventually they lost its support.

UNP fosters language and ethnic divide

Towards the next elections, the UNP once again played the 'race card'. The first victim of this strategy was the Tamil Congress which was in alliance with the UNP. The All Ceylon Tamil Congress (ACTC) worked with the UNP in its attacks on the workers. GG Ponnampalam, who had defended the UNP during the strike, was also forced by the new administration to resign. The UNP government returned to their old ways and attacked the rights of the plantation workers.

The Nehru-Kotelawala Pact, signed on 18 January 1954, denounced the democratic rights of the plantation Tamils and, using the age-old Kandyan antagonism, was an attempt to win the support of the Sinhala masses. The Pact was an agreement whereby India took responsibility for the plantation Tamils, giving the pretence that the 'stateless' workers would have their problems sorted out. This was not to be the case.

Only a few of the Tamil elite leaders understood that many Tamils, regardless of whether they were plantation workers, Muslims or other, could easily be made stateless. The Tamil leaders failed to understand the significance of the reference in the pact to the Tamil language as an 'Indian language'.

In India, under the constitution of 1950, Hindi was made an official language. But, the Indian constitution recognised all languages spoken in India as national languages. Even though not openly stated at the time by the UNP government, the UNP began to prepare the argument that Sinhala was to be the national language of Ceylon.

The government was wary on this issue as, for a long time the LSSP had argued that both Sinhala and Tamil should be the island's national languages instead of English. The UNP was careful not to give support to the LSSP demands.

With the experience of the solidarity shown in the general strike of 1953, John Kotelawala was aware that the LSSP, with the support of all sections of workers, was growing to be a major force in the country. It had massive support among the plantation workers and had organised a union for them. Like his predecessors, Kotelawala calculated that an attack on this oppressed group of workers would be a blow against the LSSP. He was ready to employ communalism, racism and any other divisive tactic to break the solidarity that the LSSP was achieving.

Kotelawala's intention was disclosed in a comment he made at the time, in which he revealed his ultimate aim: "If even the devil wanted to fight communism, I would be on his side".

Sinhala nationalism was kept at bay by the workers' movement. But the right achieved one major breakthrough. On his visit to the north, John Kotelawala, without realising what the impact would be, stated that 'Parity of Status' would be given to Tamils. To the right-wing communalists this presented a long-awaited opportunity. They claimed that all Sinhalese would be forced to learn Tamil! The Sinhala nationalists rose in opposition. They unleashed lies and rumours such as the country had not heard before. In the communalists' view, the UNP, quite correctly, deprived the plantation workers of voting rights and they argued that this deprivation should apply to all 'foreigners' including the Tamils in the north and east who claimed the historical land of the Sinhala people. Anagarika Dharmapala's views and the historical victories against the Tamil kings were rediscovered. The Kandyan convention of 1815 was remembered.

The worldwide celebrations of the 2,500th anniversary of the parinibbana (death) of the Buddha in 1956 provided the monks and the nationalists with the opportunity and platform for spreading their propaganda. The SLFP saw the celebrations as a chance to give the communalists a chance to express themselves politically and for the party to thereby gain the support of the Sinhala majority. They mixed Sinhala nationalism with populism. SWRD Bandaranaike declared that Sinhala should be the only language in the country and pledged that were he elected at the next election, he would make Sinhala and only Sinhala, the national language.

Some UNP leaders who had watched with horror as their members rallied behind the SLFP, also decided to jump on the bandwagon. The UNP reversed its position on the language question and promised to safeguard the Sinhala language better than the SLFP would. As a result of this promise, all the Tamil MPs in the UNP resigned. But these Tamil MPs had learnt nothing about defending the rights of all Tamils. They did not see that the attack on the workers and the plantation Tamils was an attack on all oppressed and all minorities. Time and again they sought an alliance with the UNP. Their behaviour is a typical example of class politics. The aspirations of the Tamil capitalists had more in common with those of their Sinhala counterparts in the UNP than with the poor Tamil masses. It was a case of class collaboration against the workers, be they Sinhala, Tamil or Muslim.

Neither John Kotelawala nor the UNP expected the Sinhala nationalist uprising of 1955. Until then, despite divisions and nationalist campaigns, almost all the parties had stood for equal rights for both languages, at least on paper. But all that changed suddenly and the leading parties began to ride on the rising wave of nationalism. Sinhala nationalist mobs attacked Tamil and Sinhala meetings held in support of equal rights. At one of the LSSP's public meetings a bomb was thrown at Reginald Medis who was guarding the entrance to meeting. He lost his hand in that attack. Mob violence spread across the country and continued throughout the election in 1956 and after.

The Tri Sinhala Peramuna, headed by JR Jayewardene, was accused of being the mastermind behind the mobs. Jayewardene used the situation to attack the left and employed organised mobs to physically take on political opponents. He also used the situation to increase his popularity among the rural Sinhala elite.

Later, in the late 1970s and early 1980s, when he became, first, prime minister, then president, he was again to put to use the lessons he had learnt about what could be gained through communal violence.

In 1955, NM Perera had attacked Jayewardene's propaganda in parliament, accusing him of sponsoring the Tri Sinhala Peramuna-organised mobs. He said: "Sinhala alone will form, not a Ceylonese nation, but a Sinhalese nation". JR Jayewardene interrupted his speech shouting "you are speaking in English". But NM Perera went on: "It is not enough for us merely to mouth phrases and say that the minority communities have nothing to fear from the majority community; that in the past we have all got on well, and that we will get on in the same old way. That is not enough today. Today the situation has gone beyond that. Today we have to do something positive in order to ally these fears that are increasing. What is worse, if we do not take a positive stand, we will continue to give room for Sinhalese chauvinists to do what damage they can."

Delivered on 19 October 1955, it was an incredible speech for the time. However it fell on deaf ears. Having tasted popularity, neither the SLFP nor the UNP was prepared to give up their nationalistic stands.

The 1956 election was decisive. The MEP (People's United Front with the SLFP - also known as the 'language front' (Sinhala)) formed the government with 51 seats. The LSSP, despite internal problems came second with 14 seats. The Federal Party won ten seats. But the most significant change was the reduction of the UNP's vote from 54 seats in the previous election to just eight seats. The Tamil Congress won only one seat.

This result for the LSSP was a significant statement against nationalism. However, Sinhala and Tamil nationalism did attract major victories for the SLFP and the FP, exposing the rift already taking place. The MEP coalition's victory represented, in some ways, a shift to the left. Despite alienating minorities, the coalition stood for nationalisation and, also, for reforms that workers could relate to.

Language act and the rise of communalism

SWRD Bandaranaike kept his promise. On 5 June 1956, the Sinhala-only Language Act was passed and became law but was not to be implemented until 1961. The passing of the Act had set the scene for civil war.

On the day the Act was passed, over 300 people attended a sit-in Satyagraha near the parliament. The sit-in was attacked by violent mobs. The violence spread to the Tamil areas. Shops and houses were burnt. In Gal Oya in the eastern province, a mob massacred over 150 Tamils. A short while after, Tamils were again attacked, including those living in the east (Ambarai and Batticoloa). Many Tamils who lived in Colombo fled to the north. Some left the country for India and other parts of the world.

Before this period, the Federal Party had not been the strongest party, representing only the petit bourgeois layer and the elite among the Tamils. In the 1952 elections, it only managed to gain 45,331 votes and two seats. In 1956, with anti-Tamil feeling at an all-time high, the Federal Party got 142,758 votes, winning ten seats. The Tamil capitalist class still voted for the UNP. However, the Sinhala-only Act and the 1956 riots changed the character of the Federal Party. Rising Sinhala nationalism helped the Federal Party to consolidate Tamil nationalism. The Tamil leaders of the time did not have a true perspective of the situation nor or any worked out programme on how to safeguard the interest of the minorities. Their electoral-based programmes had no coherent strategy. Despite, from time to time, raising the idea of a 'separate country' for Tamils, they represented divergent views and were confused about how best to deal with the attacks on Tamils.

With the rise of Tamil nationalism, all divisions among Tamils based on caste and religion were pushed back. For the first time, the Federal Party attracted Tamil-speaking Muslim youth and young people from the oppressed castes. However, the Federal Party leadership did not have the vision or the capacity to offer leadership to the youth who joined the party, impatient for change. Instead, it had several meetings with the government.

With the LSSP and other left leaders campaigning for 'minority rights', SWRD Bandaranaike feared that if he did not respond to the communal tensions, he might lose the support of the workers. Southern workers called a strike in which more than 80,000 participated. The UNP, which had taken an extreme right-wing, pro-Sinhala Buddhist nationalist stand, providing a platform for the communalists, attacked the striking workers. In 1957 Bandaranaike postponed the implementation of the Sinhala-only Act and came to an agreement with the Federal Party. The agreement he signed with SJV Chelvanayagam, the leader of the Federal Party, in July 1957, the 'Banda-Chelva Pact', caused another wave of uproar among the Sinhala nationalists. The UNP used the election as an opportunity to provide a national base for communal outcries.

In September 1957 the notorious UNP right-winger, JR Jayewardene announced that, in opposition to the Pact, he would march from Colombo to the sacred Buddhist temple, Sri Dalada Maligawa, in Kandy.

All the other parties opposed the UNP's stand. The LSSP organised barricades to prevent the march. All the way to Kandy, marchers were physically stopped by the organised opposition of Sinhala workers. Jayewardene managed to smuggle himself to the Dalada Maligawa in a vehicle and took a much-publicised oath to oppose the Pact. Neither Junius Richard Jayewardene nor Solomon West Ridgeway Dias Bandaranaike was Buddhist by birth. It was neither love of religion nor of language that led them to take this Buddhist nationalist stand. Rather it was their struggle for power for the benefit of themselves and their class.

Only a few years previously in 1953 the workers had shown great solidarity and willingness to fight to change society along anti-capitalist and socialist lines. Many workers and poor people had rejected the UNP - the traditional party of the capitalists. Manipulation of the reactionary elements by means of the language question did not have an impact among politically conscious workers. In fact, the majority of the workers could not understand how the Sinhala-only Act could be implemented. Those who worked in government offices knew that implementation of the Act would not be practical. The majority of poor workers and farmers in the Tamil-speaking areas did not speak Sinhala nor, or for that matter, English. Even when English was the official language, workers used Tamil in the Tamil areas and Sinhala in the Sinhala areas. As the LSSP pointed out it, it made sense to make both languages national languages.

But the real battle was for government jobs – the government was the largest employer and government jobs meant high status in society. Middle class Sinhalese and Tamils competed for these jobs. The Sinhala-only Act ensured that the majority of the government jobs would go to Sinhala workers. The situation had not been anticipated by the Tamil capitalist class and petit bourgeoisie.

The Act divided the country along communal lines in a way that could not be repaired without addressing the emergent Tamil nationalism and making some concessions to it.

In the riots that followed the passing of the Act, over 1,000 Tamils were killed and thousands made homeless. Despite the state of emergency which had been declared, organised mobs attacked Tamil houses and shops while the police watched. JR Jayewardene was accused – even by right-wing politicians – of being the mastermind behind the organised mobs.

With pressure from the Buddhist monks mounting, SWRD Bandaranaike capitulated. On 9 April 1958, he publicly tore up the Banda-Chelva Pact and gave written promises to the monks that he would not implement it. Leading Ilankai Tamil Arasu Kadchi (ITAK or the Federal Party, FP) members were arrested. Along with the spontaneous protests in Tamil areas, the LSSP organised a series of meetings. SWRD Bandaranaike was trapped between the workers struggling for their rights and the communalists rioting for their privileges. When the Language Act was passed on 14 August 1958, fearing a workers' revolt, Bandaranike made a few concessions.

However, the LSSP kept up the pressure on the language issue. In protest, some left forces within the SLFP left the government coalition. Frustrated monks began a campaign against the left within the SLFP. The monks had more than one reason, locally and internationally, for mounting a campaign. While the SLFP worked closely with the Chinese government, that government's attack on Tibet in 1958 had outraged the Buddhist leaders in Sri Lanka. But no one could have foreseen the lengths to which the Buddhist leaders were prepared to take their attacks. On 25 September 1959, a Buddhist monk, called Talduwe Somaram, visited SWRD Bandaranaike and fired a gun at point blank range at him. The assassination was the first high-profile political murder in Sri Lanka. A few Buddhist nationalists who had funded the SLFP election campaign were found guilty of the murder. There was total confusion within the LSSP. A vote of no-confidence later led to the dissolution of parliament and a new election was called for 19 March 1960.

In the new election no party obtained a clear majority and a hung parliament emerged. The SLFP, now led by Srimavo Bandaranaike, SWRD's widow, sought the support of ITAK, promising to implement the Banda-Chelva Pact. Chelvanayakam, after meeting with Srimavo, agreed to support the SLFP. But the right-wing parties, in the hope of forming a majority government, demanded a new election.

After the governor cleverly avoided giving the SLFP the opportunity to form a new government an election was held in July of the same year. (The governor was later found guilty of attempting a military coup to overthrow the SLFP government.) The SLFP emerged with 75 seats and a clear victory. The UNP managed just 30 seats. ITAK won 12 seats. The LSSP managed only 12 seats, a major defeat for the supporters of the right-wing's policies.

Srimavo became the world's first female prime minister. She soon showed that she had no interest whatsoever in addressing the concerns of the minorities. Instead the Language Act was implemented. ITAK was in agreement with the government on the implementation of the Act. But their extreme right-wing approach could not bring them close to the SLFP-led government. With no support coming from the FP, the SLFP government abandoned any idea of making any concessions on the issue of the Tamil language.

1960s: an era of struggle and missed opportunities

The 1960s were a period of radicalisation of the working masses around the world. The Cuban revolution in 1959 was closely watched by workers everywhere. The war in Vietnam was very much on workers' minds. Workers and young people learned that struggle can change society and many were ready to struggle. The period is also memorable for the failures of left leaderships to put forward a programme that could channel that willingness to struggle into successful revolutions.

In Sri Lanka, the LSSP was undergoing change. Having failed to capitalise on the valorous struggle of the workers during the general strike of 1953, the leadership was struggling to retain support among workers who wanted a leadership that would stand firm on a revolutionary programme. However, by the 1960s the party had regained mass support. Its members were at the head of a number of trade unions and had led almost all the workers' struggles. In the March 1960 election it won its highest vote to date – 325,286 votes (10.5%) - despite standing in a limited number of seats. During the elections, to prevent the UNP returning to power, they agreed upon a non-aggression pact with the SLFP and with other left-leaning parties.

However, the election results do not reflect the strength of the

LSSP at that time. It had numerous branches, even in rural areas. Having earned the respect of the workers and poor masses, they were considered the strongest political force in the country. It was difficult at the time for anybody to gain the confidence of the masses without the support of the LSSP.

The LSSP defended the rights of Tamils and all workers. It was the driving force behind the campaign for nationalisation, which, to a minor extent, the Srimavo government implemented. However, it was faced with the major problem of ethnic polarisation among workers – the results of which were harvested by the right wing.

With the workers and the poor divided along ethnic lines, the LSSP was looked to for leadership by both Sinhala and Tamil workers. As founding member Leslie Goonewardene pointed out: "[The LSSP] lost heavily among the Sinhalese masses. And although it has won the sympathy of the minorities, this has far from compensated for the losses."

A leadership was needed that would take up the class issues with the aim of mobilising the workers of both groups and lead them to change society to the benefit of all. But the LSSP leaders proved incapable of producing such results. Their energies became directed mainly towards gaining election victories.

Tamil nationalism was gaining support among the Tamil masses. It was also gaining support from the Tamil bosses and rich elite. Having been attacked from all sides, the Tamil capitalist leaders were driven to take a nationalistic stand. However, they did so without consideration for the minorities or a programme for safeguarding their rights.

The leaders within the ITAK-Federal Party had no idea of how nationalism was developing. Their analysis of developments was linked to the support that the FP received on the basis of their stand for Tamil language and education rights, etc. It never went beyond their electoral ambitions. Tamil nationalism helped ITAK-Federal Party leaders to alienate the SLFP and the UNP and secured them a dominant position among the Tamils. Beyond full electoral monopoly the FP's programme was restricted to capitalist demands which were very limited. It still supported the UNP's economic policies. It did not have any alternative economic approach that would benefit ordinary Tamils.

The 1960 election also saw major defeats for some leading Tamil right-wing politicians such as GG Ponnampalam and C Suntharalingam etc. SJV Chelvanayagam, a charismatic leader of the FP, realised that he, too, would be pushed aside if he was not consistent in speaking out for Tamil rights.

For the first time a large number of young people and workers from different backgrounds joined the FP. With the influx of new members, many of whom were activists, the FP's character changed. The activists were radicals who, inspired by world events, sought social change. If the LSSP had moved to give leadership positions to them, the history of Sri Lanka might have been different. For these Tamil young people, the LSSP was just another Sinhala electoral party. The FP old guard did all it could to discredit the left leaders. The right-wing UNP leaders and the SLFP leaders were much more respected and popularised by the old FP leaders than the LSSP members who had a much better position regarding Tamil rights.

The upper-caste make-up of the FP leadership and of some of the youth leaders shaped their opposition to leftists who supported the riots and activities of the oppressed castes. V Karalasingham, a Tamil member of the LSSP, pointed out later that: "Thondaman and Chelvanayakam, each for his own class reason, successfully held back the masses who were supporting them from the LSSP".

The FP organised several protests against the implementation of the Language Act. On 2 January 1961, the first day of implementation of the Act, the FP organised a successful Hartal in Tamil areas. Independence Day on 4 February was observed as a day of mourning. The party had also decided to launch a civil disobedience campaign in February. The leadership became aware of the left proclivities of the youth and, seeking to convert them to the right, fed them false information about the Indian and western governments. And, despite the fact that large numbers of the oppressed caste had joined the party, FP leaders defended the caste system. They also looked up to the Tamil leaders in Tamil Nadu. Using pro-Gandhian propaganda and methods, a satyagraha (passive resistance) was planned and organised.

In 1960, the Dravidian movement in Tamil Nadu was at its peak. The movement had its roots in the pre-independence anti-imperialist struggle and anti-oppressive caste struggles. (The oppressor caste consisted mainly of Brahmins, who considered themselves to be Aryan, as distinct from the majority oppressed groups, the Dravidians). After independence, the Dravidian movement had adopted a strong anti-Aryan character. Strong Dravidian – comparable to Dalit - movements in the western part of India had begun to spread from the south to the rest of India.

These movements spread during the period when, attempting to escape caste oppression, large numbers of the oppressed castes abandoned Hinduism and converted to other religions. The majority, including large numbers of Tamils, became Buddhists. Dr BR Ambedkar, who was born into the oppressed caste and had become a prominent figure on the Indian political scene, had declared, in 1935, that he would not die a Hindu and urged many of his caste to convert to Buddhism. But the Stalinists, departing from Marxism, had failed to address the difficult issue of caste oppression. The people, having lost faith that so-called 'Marxists' could solve their problems, turned to Ambedkar's ideas. The Dalit movement spread at a rapid rate.

In October 1956 Ambedkar converted to Buddhism along with half a million followers. At one point in 1957, in a ceremony at Lucknow, the Sri Lankan Buddhist monks converted 15,000 people. Although the conversion to Buddhism played a role in mobilising people from the oppressed caste, it did nothing to solve the caste problem that existed. The Burmese or Sri Lankan Buddhist monks who were involved in these conversions did nothing to address the caste and economic discrimination that existed in their respective countries. Later, the movement led to the formation among the oppressed castes of strong caste-based political organisations. This in itself created new complications and provided no solutions.

In Tamil Nadu, EV Ramaswamy, (Periyar - meaning great man), also let down by the Stalinist failure to challenge caste oppression, spearheaded the movement of the oppressed castes. By the 1960s, the movement had fallen into the hands of a section of young people who saw the Dravidian movement as a revival of the Dravidian race and fostered the development of a Dravidian nationalist consciousness. Dravida Munnetra Kazhagam (DMK), a movement which, in 1949, had split away from the Dravida Kazhagam, led by CN Annadurai, came to prominence when it campaigned for a separate Tamil Nadu state, ie separate from India. The movement suffered a setback when the Indo-China War broke out in 1962. It rallied, however, and one of its major successes was its campaign against the implementation of Hindi as the language of administration in Tamil Nadu. With soaring popularity it came to power in 1967 and since then Tamil Nadu politics have been shaped by Dravidian parties.

All the leaders of the DMK had given assistance to the Tamil youth in Sri Lanka. Even though its origins were rooted in the fight against anti-caste oppression, a new version of the movement soon abandoned this approach in favour of electoral politics. Because it posed no threat to their existence, the Sri Lankan Tamil elite took pride in associating themselves with the DMK leaders.

DMK leaders were and are prominent in literary circles and in the cinema industry and their popularity has spread through art and culture. MG Ramachandiran (MGR for short) was Tamil Nadu's most famous politician and a famous actor. The majority of the films starring MGR were packed with pro-Dravidian rhetoric. These films were most successful, not only in the north and east of Sri Lanka, but also in the south. At that time Tamil Nadu cinema and music was dominant in Sri Lanka and were also watched and listened to by the Sinhala masses. Supporters of Dravidian nationalism include Annadurai, a famous novelist who became the first DMK chief minister in Tamil Nadu, and M Karunanithi, a famous poet and screenplay writer who also served as chief minister on five occasions and remains in control of the DMK until now. All this fame helped the separatist mood in the north of Sri Lanka. In the south, however, it served to strengthen the Sinhala nationalist slander against the Tamil minorities.

When the FP leaders turned to the DMK leaders in Tamil Nadu for help, the move was welcomed by the Tamil masses. A Satyagraha organised by the FP was supported by the plantation workers. This act of solidarity was significant. Previously, the Tamil elite, due to their role in supporting right-wing policies against the plantation Tamils, had never been able to win the support of the workers. The Satyagrha was the first sign that Tamil nationalism was taking centre stage among wider sections of the Tamil-speaking people in the country.

A decision by the FP to issue federal stamps at the post offices – with the first stamp issued by Chelvanayagam to popularise the demand for separation – was proscribed by the Srimavo government. A state of emergency was declared and a number of FP leaders were arrested and detained for six months. The military moved in to control the government offices and post offices. The military had been used by the UNP government during the 1953 general strike to escort the scab workers and guard the ports, etc. By now it had become common practice to use the military against trade unions and striking workers. The LSSP vigorously opposed this practice as they saw it, correctly, as an attack on all workers. But they failed to understand the Tamil nationalist movement that was taking shape.

The LSSP, quite correctly, noted that the FP leaders were all upper caste and from privileged backgrounds while the large numbers of youth who were willing to fight were often from poor families and from the oppressed castes. The LSSP predicted a youth revolt against the upper caste leaders and imagined that they would then be able to organise the struggling Tamil workers alongside Sinhala workers.

This was a gross underestimation of the growth of Tamil nationalism. Not having proposed a solution to the discrimination faced by these youth, the LSSP had no chance of organising them. Ignoring this issue was to prove fatal, not just for the party, but also for the future of the youth movement which fell into the hands of the right-wing nationalists.

It is important to emphasise here that the Tamil-speaking masses – from the Jaffna elite and the upper caste Tamils, to the Tamils in the east, and the oppressed castes, to Muslims, plantation workers, Indian workers and even Burghers of Tamil origin – were all united in disagreement with the government position on the language question. The left was in unison with them. However, the LSSP, in fear of losing the support of the Sinhala working masses, and the FP, in fear of losing its grip among the Tamils, did not acknowledge the importance of working together towards a solution to the minority question.

The LSSP, having characterised the FP as a capitalist party, relied on Tamil FP members –a quite significant number at the time – to take their work forward among the Tamil masses. But the LSSP failed to understand the dissatisfaction felt even among its own ranks on the language question. Tamil members of the LSSP wanted the LSSP to take a bold step and lead the way in the struggle to defend their rights – which they thought that the FP was doing.

If the LSSP had taken a strong position on the national question they definitely would have won mass support among the Tamils. But they wrongly feared they would lose the support of the Sinhala workers. Their inability to solve this 'riddle' still haunts the party.

Later, having agreed to form a coalition government with the SLFP, the LSSP modified its position on the issue of parity status for the Tamil language and reduced it to a demand for the right for it to be a regional language. The LSSP began to lose its Tamil membership.

On the other hand, SLFP policies, such as subsidies to small farmers, promotion of small scale industry, etc, began to make an impact on the lives of ordinary workers. Poor farmers and the members of the oppressed castes began, for the first time, to experience benefits.

Like SWRD Bandaranaike, Srimavo feared the most powerful force in the country – the working class. Strikes and political discussions took place in workplaces. Political activism among the youth and students increased. Sinhala workers and youth in the south took to the streets to demand more rights. This was a period of change – and of lost opportunity!

The prime minister, facing a constant wave of strikes, declared a state of emergency. A strike by bank employees was declared illegal. But, soon afterwards, the Ceylon Transport Board was paralysed by a six-day strike. LSSP-led trade unions supported that strike, soon to be joined by the Colombo dock workers. By the end of 1961, over 17,000 workers were on strike at the port. A general strike was called for 5 January 1962. Despite the army and the navy moving in to operate the services, the general strike was deemed to be very successful. The government had been forced to concede to the main demands of the workers.

Thus pushed from below, the Srimavo government leaned to the left. In 1961, within a year of the election, the Bank of Ceylon was nationalised. The government also nationalised the assets of the petroleum companies and insurance corporations. The British and United States governments immediately enforced an aid embargo.

In the same way as the Tamil nationalists had underestimated the growing strength of the Tamil masses, the Sinhala nationalists deluded themselves into believing that they were in control of the Sinhalese people. In reality, the support both parties received was the expression of the masses' desire to change society. Beneath the polarisation along ethnic lines was the underlying struggle of both sections for better living conditions: housing, education, etc – solid demands. The LSSP failed to respond to these needs as the FP pushed them to the right. In contrast, Srimavo, aware of the masses' objectives, was able to gain support by implementing some worker-friendly policies. Both Sinhala and Tamil people benefitted from the implementation of such policies.

Betrayal of the workers' movement – fall of the LSSP

Stalin's death in 1953 led to changes in the foreign policies of the Soviet Union. In 1961 the Chinese government publicly denounced the Soviets as 'traitors', and intense debates and discussions were sparked among the left around the world. The Sino-Soviet split had divided the Communist Parties internationally. A revolutionary wave was sweeping the world. In Pakistan, for example, the masses had begun their struggle.

In 1961 the Indian prime minister announced that the country had the technology to make atomic bombs. With India's war with China, which broke out in 1962, the arms race was intensified. The Cold War, as played out in Asia and Africa was gaining momentum while the US was sponsoring coups and attacks against many left governments.

The questioning of Stalinism, the methods and ideas propounded by the leadership of the USSR, had a major impact, particularly in the neocolonial world. The revolutionary wave in Poland, Hungary, France and Portugal, Cuba and Chile and elsewhere around the world provided hope for the workers and poor and the impetus to fight back. But above all, for the struggling masses in the colonies, the Cuban revolution provided inspiration. Che Guevara was an international celebrity.

Throughout the 1960s, taking inspiration from Cuba and China, the Naxalbari movement spread across India. Guerrilla tactics became common. The Sino-Soviet debate and the debate and discussion that followed within the Fourth International also had an impact.

In Sri Lanka, the LSSP was misled by the leaders of the Fourth International. At a time when fast-developing workers' movements were most in need of inspired leadership, the Fourth International was divided on tactics and on the direction workers' movements should take. Nevertheless, the LSSP announced that its progress was unparalleled in history.

In 1962, the Srimavo government faced a right-wing military coup attempt which, due to a tip-off, was avoided at the last minute. Although militancy was growing among Sinhala, Muslim and Tamil youth, the LSSP decided that: "it would be difficult to evoke that degree of militancy among the workers necessary for extra-parliamentary actions". A group within the LSSP saw Srimavo's economic policies as semi-revolutionary and argued in support of those policies. One leading member of the group, NM Perera, wrote a document urging the LSSP to change its policies and tactics.

He thought that the LSSP was unlikely to succeed "within the conceivable future in getting its policy and programme accepted by a significant number of people to enable it to attain power through parliamentary means". This premise led to a debate about the pros and cons of coalition with the SLFP and, in turn, raised questions about the character of the SLFP. Left-wing Sama Samajists argued vigorously against a coalition of any sort. Having characterised the SLFP as a capitalist party just a few months previously, the LSSP now came to the conclusion that it was a 'reformist petit-bourgeois party' and "capitalist only in the sense that its ultimate objective is not an overthrow of capitalism".

The Sino-Soviet debate split the Ceylon Communist party (CCP). In 1963, N Sanmugathasan, its leading member, and many others who had been expelled from the CCP, formed the CCP-Maoist (Peking Wing). A young Sinhala man named Patabendi Don Nandasiri Wijeweera (alias Rohana Wijeweera), returned from the Soviet Union and, critical of the policies of the Soviet Union, joined the Wing. Later, in 1969, Rohana Wijeweera founded the Janatha Vimukthi Peramuna (JVP), the People's Liberation Front.

Sanmugathasan, being a Tamil, made an immediate impact on the Tamils. His party swung into action and led revolts of the oppressed castes in Changanai and many other rural towns in the north.

At the time, Tamil workers were looking for a left alternative. In Tamil areas, such as Chunnakam, Manipay, Uduvil, Anaikotai, and Puloli, the left (LSSP and CP) led the town councils. The teachers' union, the General Clerical Services Union (GCSU), the bank and mercantile unions, the transport workers' union, the cigar workers' unions, all had Tamil majorities and close links with the left. These unions had participated in the 1953 general strike in solidarity with Sinhala workers. But heightened fear of ethnic discrimination and of Sinhala nationalism began to alienate a number of their members.

Leading leftists in these unions and councils took a position against the caste system and defended the rights of the oppressed caste during the caste riots. These leftists aroused the hostility of the Federal Party. When a number of communal-based 'Tamil trade unions' emerged, partly to defend the workers' rights and partly due to a lack of trust in some Sinhala nationalist trade unionists, the Federal Party took the opportunity to push them to the right. Within the Tamil workers' movement, an upper caste leadership slowly emerged, which allied itself to the FP leadership.

By 1963 the LSSP, the CP, and the MEP had begun talks on a united front. On May Day, they held a joint rally and on 8 August, they formally agreed to form the United Left Front (ULF). The 16-point programme adopted by the ULF changed the LSSP's positions on economic reforms and on the language and citizenship rights of the minorities. Whereas the LSSP's 1960 election manifesto had omitted any demand for parity status for the Tamil language, the ULF announced that it endorsed the Official Language Act of 1956 and the Tamil Language Special Provisions Act of 1958. They also took a step back on the right to citizenship of the plantation workers, which, as the government had announced its decision to stop employing stateless persons in government services, was devastating to these workers. However the LSSP managed, despite opposition from the MEP, to get the ULF to agree to demands for additional rights for the stateless by removing administrative difficulties. But, overall, this compromise further alienated the Tamil masses from the LSSP.

At the same time the Srimavo government was under great pressure from the workers. Strikes started in December 1963 and continued all the way through 1964. Postal workers, electrical engineers and government medical officers went on strike. The government attempted to clamp down on the strikers by declaring a state of emergency which caused more floods of protest. The government also faced a vote of no-confidence from the ULF. By the end of March the government signalled that it would negotiate with the ULF with a view to establishing some cooperation. In May, NM Perera, who worked as a chief negotiator, declared that the ULF would join the SLFP government.

Srimavo informed her party that: "The leftists who worked with us began a series of strikes because they did not get a place in the government. In the north... there were communal issues flaring up. Some people have various ideas on these subjects, some feel that these workers can be made to work at the point of a gun and bayonet. Still others maintain that a national government should be formed to solve these problems. I have considered these ideas separately and in the context of world events. My conclusion is that none of these solutions will take us where we want to go. Therefore, gentlemen, I decided to initiate talks with the leaders of the working class, particularly with Mr Philip Gunawardene and Dr NM Perera."

Turbulent splits and fights among the leading factions within the LSSP followed. Fourteen members of the central committee, including Edmund Samarakkody, Bala Tampoe, V Karalasingham, passed a resolution against the coalition and decided to form the

LSSP (revolutionary section) after walking out of the conference which adopted the LSSP-SLFP coalition. LSSP members obtained three ministerial posts. NM Perera (finance), Anil Moonesinghe (communications), Cholmondely Goonewardene (public works). The LSSP was expelled from the Fourth International.

When Jawaharlal Nehru, the Indian prime minister, died on 27 May 1964 the Indian political scene began to change rapidly. On 30 October 1964, the Srimavo government delegation signed an agreement with Delhi regarding the stateless workers and the poor. The Indian government agreed to take back the majority of them – around 525,000 people, a truly despicable act. Srimavo justified the agreement on the grounds that: "The upcountry people lost their political rights as a result of the election of Indian MPs to the seats where the Indian plantation workers predominated. These Indian plantation workers are a group of people who have received more wages and... great privileges. The Indian workers got this better treatment from the very start; they are now enhancing it through their trade unions to an extent far exceeding what they have produced. The peasantry of the upcountry areas is at present subjected to this foreign exploitation."

The Tamil Nadu people were outraged by this agreement. CN Annadurai, the DMK leader in Tamil Nadu, gave lengthy speeches against it. With opposition mounting, Srimavo began to lose support among her party members. After losing a vote of no-confidence the government was dissolved and an election called in March 1965.

The character of the FP was soon made clear to the Tamil youth. In the course of that election, the FP made a secret agreement with the UNP. Thondaman of the Ceylon Workers Congress (CWC), the self-appointed representative of the plantation workers, also lived up to his class reputation and made an agreement with the UNP.

The rhetoric of the so-called Tamil leaders at the time matched that of the Buddhist Sinhala nationalists. These Hindu nationalists reinvented the historic victories of the Tamil Kings and boasted about Dravidian culture and its domination. Some FP leaders, such as Amirthalingam, gave rousing speeches attacking 'Sinhalese' people as an inferior race. This Hindu self-praise failed to win them new support. In fact they lost their only two seats in the 1965 election. The UNP made gains and won 66 seats. The SLFP won 41 seats and the LSSP won ten seats, a loss of two seats.

The UNP, unable to win an outright majority, was forced to rely on the FP and the CWC (Thondaman) to form a government. The

SLFP attempts to negotiate with the FP failed as the FP leaders preferred to associate themselves with the UNP rather than with the SLFP or any other left party, even though, in doing so, they had to compromise their demands. To keep the FP on side, UNP leader Dudley Senanayake came to an arrangement with SJV Chelvanayakam and, on 24 March 1965, a Pact was signed. The Pact was a whitewash agreement that suited only the FP and UNP leaders – it was a 'marriage of convenience'. All the points requested by the FP in the agreement were either already implemented or in the process of being implemented by the SLFP government. At this stage, the LSSP stood for more far-going rights for Tamils than the FP. Had the FP genuinely cared for the rights of the Tamils they could easily have seen through the UNP and chosen to follow a path that, in the long run, would have been better for the minorities. Instead they selfishly prioritised their own careers!

The UNP formed a government with the support of five other parties; the Federal Party, the All-Ceylon Tamil Congress (ACTC), the Sri Lanka Freedom Socialist Party (SLFSP), the Mahajana Ekseth Perumuna (MEP), the Ceylon Workers Congress (CWC) as well as with the independents. A committee of ten was formed under the leadership of UNP members; Dudley Senanayake and JR Jayewardene. Both men had been instrumental in organising a communal march to Kandy demanding the implementation of the Language Act and were active in the anti-Tamil riots.

It soon became clear what the FP wanted. The first political act of Mr Tiruchelvam, new minister of Local Government and the only Tamil minister in the UNP government, was to dissolve the Jaffna Municipality over a dispute with its mayor, Alfred Duraiyappah, who wanted the Tamil Matha statue to be erected in front of Jaffna library. Tamil Hindu rhetoric prevailed. Arumuga Navalar, the Hindu revivalist and a cynical defender of the caste system, was declared a national hero and his statue was taken, in a large procession, from Colombo to Jaffna where it was re-erected.

While the FP leaders were involved in politics in Colombo, a rift was occurring within the party. The MP for Kayts, V Navaratnam, broke away from the party and called for self-government. He was the only Tamil MP in the coalition who had opposed the passing of the Indo-Ceylon Bill which denied citizenship to half a million plantation Tamils. The FP leader, Chelvanayakam, had persuaded Navaratnam to absent himself from parliament while the Bill was being passed with the support of the FP.

In reaction to the FP's upper caste politics in the north, the oppressed caste rose against the landlords and others of the oppressing caste. The 'Temple Entry' riots of 1968 were significant. Young people, Jaffna university students in particular, played an important part in the riots. The CPC (Maoist) of Sanmugathasan also played a significant part, thereby winning a number of recruits. Socialist ideas were taking centre stage among the youth and struggling masses in the north, but, criminally, the LSSP failed to appeal to them.

A non-violent protest was held in Maviddapuram Kandaswamy Temple to allow the oppressed caste into the temple. Meanwhile one of the main demands of the FP was to make certain temples, such as the Thirukoneswaram Temple in Trincomalee, sacred Hindu areas! A drama dealing with this issue, called Kanthan Karunai (mercy of Lord Muruga), was an instant hit among students and the youth in general. Protesters were violently attacked by the defenders of Saivism – upper caste thugs – who attacked with metal bars. None of the political parties came to the aid of the protesters. A battle also broke out in Changanai. While some pro-FP communal 'Tamil trade union' leaders were silent, several trade unionists and other left activists intervened on behalf of the oppressed castes. Meanwhile, discontent with the left leadership grew among Sinhala youth in the rural areas.

During the UNP's rule, the FP members of the parliament voted with the UNP on all their right-wing measures. During Srimavo's government the FP had opposed nationalisation including the nationalisation of schools. Of course the nationalisation was very limited and did not result in workers' control. And many workers lost their jobs. However this is not the reason why the FP opposed nationalisation. Certain rhetoric notwithstanding, they opposed nationalisation in principle because their policies were fundamentally big business-friendly. But now they even voted for the introduction of ID cards which meant that all citizens over the age of 18 had to register with a government office which, in turn issued them with a photo card. In fact, V Navaratnam was expelled from the FP for opposing this bill. FP leaders began to lose their grip on the Tamil youth. One prominent FP leader, Amirthalingam, was dubbed the 'cardboard Hitler'; even his colleagues, such as C Rajadurai, regarded him as such.

The District Council Bill, drafted by Thiruchelvam, was, also, an indirect means of implementing the Language Act. The ensuing

Sinhala communal opposition was due more to the fact that it was drafted by a Tamil minister rather than to strong objections to its content. Despite the intimidation of the poor and the compromising of workers' rights, Thiruchelvam only resigned as minister in November 1968 when, due to pressure from Buddhist monks, he was asked to suspend the declaration of Thirukoneswaram Temple as a Hindu sacred place. In his address announcing the suspension, he stated that the prime minister's action "brought to nought the unanimous wish of all Hindu religious bodies". In the following month, the FP withdrew from the national government.

The UNP also implemented right-wing policies. With prices rising, it halved the rice ration subsidy. And the poor once again faced the suppression of their rights. In the subsequent riots that broke out, communal racist elements began to take centre stage. "Dudleyge Bade Masala Vadey", literally, 'Dudley has eaten vadai' (a traditional Tamil food) was shouted in the streets, meaning 'Dudley has given in to Tamil demands'. Prices rose, inflation soared. Simultaneously, unemployment increased. Yet, while the economy was suffering, JR Jayewardene managed to pay the US government around $5.5 million in compensation for the nationalisation of American oil companies by the previous Srimavo government.

Across the southern part of the country, a number of communal parties, such as the 'Ape Sinhale' ('We Sinhalese' group), were formed. Even within the left, nationalist elements broke away to form Sinhala nationalist parties. [Already explained the formation of JVP] Rohana Wijaweera, who was expelled by Sanmugathasan, allegedly for refusing to print more Tamil leaflets, had formed a Sinhala extremist party called the Janath☒ Vimukthi Peramua (JVP - People's Liberation Front).

With the influence of the Cuban victory, the example of Che Guevara and the Chinese 'Great Leap Forward' very much to the fore, the JVP went underground to undertake guerrilla training. Within the LSSP, NM Perera was winning the argument for a broader coalition. In 1968, the LSSP, CP and SLFP came together again to form a so-called united front and agreed on a 'common programme'.

This time, with the influence of the LSSP, the coalition adopted several progressive demands. It stood for land reform, extensive nationalisation, and the setting up of a new constituent assembly. This programme can still be considered the most progressive programme that any major Sri Lankan party or coalition ever proposed. The LSSP argued that the programme was a step towards creating favourable conditions for a socialist revolution. With this programme they were able, once again, under the banner of struggle, to bring together the powerful Sri Lankan working class. Despite communal riots and the rhetoric of some left nationalists, this broader coalition won the support of thousands of workers in all parts of the country. The 1970 May Day rally is said to have been the largest May Day event of all time in the country.

With the forthcoming elections, the FP, after a long-standing collaboration with the UNP involving compromise and betrayal of the interests of the workers, the ordinary poor and minority groups, took a further turn to the right. In their election manifesto, they stated that they stood for federalism and demanded autonomy as a step towards a federation. They justified their actions on the grounds of working towards these goals. But voters, who had given them the benefit of the doubt in the last election, had learnt that their leaders had abused their trust and it had cost them dear. The only appeal the FP's election strategy had was to the Tamil Hindu nationalists.

More on the election FP and LSSP

The 1970 election resulted in a major victory for the left. Under Srimavo, the SLFP, with 106 seats, won 49% of the vote and, with six seats from the CP, formed the government. The LSSP won 19 seats with 433,224 votes, the largest vote obtained by any Trotskyist party in the world. Meanwhile the UNP suffered a major defeat, managing to win only 17 seats, fewer than the LSSP. The FP maintained its voting base, winning 13 seats. However its key leaders suffered their worst defeats ever. A Amirthalingam, M Sivasithamparam, GG Ponnampalam all lost their seats.

LSSP leaders were given ministerial positions: Dr NM Perera (Finance minister), Leslie Gunewardene (Communication minister) Colvin R De Silva (minister for the Plantation Industry), Peter GB Keuneman (minister for housing and Construction). Chelliah Kumarasuriar, a Tamil, was appointed minister of Post and Telecommunication.

Dissatisfied youth, particularly in the universities, began to search for an alternative way to fight back. Soon after its victory the Srimavo government released Rohana Wijeweera, the JVP leader and other political prisoners from prison. With boosted confidence the JVP began to organise the students. It had support in the major universities. The number of youth in the JVP outnumbered that in any other political organisation of the time.

JVP insurrection

In 1971 their preparations for an uprising were leaked and Srimavo reacted immediately, giving powers to the military and police to attack and arrest JVP members. Soon several JVP leaders including Rohana Wijaweera were arrested and their weapons confiscated. On 5 April, while the arrests were in progress, the JVP, under instruction from Wijaweera in Jaffna jail, attacked the police stations.

JVP cadres captured many police stations in large areas of the south and west and managed to bring them under their control. Srimavo and her UF colleagues escaped to a ship in fear of the JVP over-running the prime minister's residence. They also called for India and other countries to help. Srimavo openly acknowledged that they were ill-equipped to face an insurrection. The Indian government responded quickly by sending troops to capture the airports, harbour, etc.

India's response strengthened the JVP's contention that that country had adopted a policy of 'Indian expansionism'. (One of the JVP's series of lectures to the cadres was on 'Indian expansionism', a confused nationalist approach to regional politics which is still used by them today).

Pakistan and other countries also helped Srimavo's government suppress the uprising. These army operations constituted the first bloodbath in Sri Lanka. Within one month over 20,000 Sinhala youth were murdered and around 20,000 were imprisoned. This brutal suppression has had long-standing consequences. It weakened the future struggle of the workers. It also helped to strengthen the state's power. The right-wing UNP was able to use the incident to threaten workers. For the first time, the military and security forces were strengthened.

The LSSP defended the government's brutality. There was no remorse. It dismissed the JVP's action as a 'misguided adventure' and declared a revolution cannot be achieved in 24 hours. They justified the military suppression and defended the government's treatment of prisoners. Its response sealed the LSSP's fate among students and other youth.

Rohana Wijaweera's statement to the court stands in stark contrast to some of the LSSP leaders' approach. His statement highlighted the reasons for the party's subsequent stagnation: He said:

"In the urban working class and the estates the influence of the Old Left was still traditions of the Sri Lanka Freedom Party (SLFP) were strongest. The SLFP won most of its seats in the rural areas. The worst massacres during the April incidents took place in the areas held by the SLFP. The SLFP politicians had shamelessly sown the germs of communal discord against the Tamil minority. In the 1956 election the CP and the LSSP stood for parity on the language issue. But what did they do a short time later? They were not only against equal status for Tamil and Sinhala, but opposed even the granting of any lesser rights. It was in these conditions that we became disillusioned with them. That is why we struggled. If anyone willingly risks his or her life, or is prepared to be shackled as a prisoner, this can only be because there is no alternative."

In contrast, the determination and commitment of the JVP made its impact, not only on Sinhala youth, but also on Tamil youth. There was increasing frustration with the FP leaders.

Despite attacking the LSSP for not providing an acceptable alternative, the JVP did not, itself, have a clear programme on issues, such as land reform, etc. In particular, due to their rejection of a demand for the right to self-determination and lack of understanding of how to solve the national question as outlined by Lenin, it failed to attract the Tamil youth. It was unable to instruct its members on the dangers of Sinhala nationalism and of chauvinism. A number of its recruits came from rural areas in the south who, in the past, had, in one way or other, been influenced by the racist propaganda of the monks and the Sinhala nationalists.

The JVP sought to use the opportunity created by the LSSP betrayal to expand its influence, but failed to adopt a Marxist programme to take the struggle forward. Its premise was based on a simplified amalgam of Stalinist and Maoist ideas tinged with Sinhala nationalism. Its leaders did not express any views on international developments, nor on the state of the international working class. They made no reference to developments within the working class in the region, not even to the struggle of the Indian working class against its state. They linked the core of their propaganda to the dangers of Indian expansionism without any attempt to provide information on the struggle the Indian working class was waging again the Indian state.

Concentrating on Indian nationalism without any reference to intra-national conflicts, was one way the JVP furthered their aim of gaining the support of Sri Lanka nationalists. To this day, the JVP, although it uses Marxist phraseology, remains by and large, a predominantly nationalist party.

FP Failure and discontent grows among youth

When, in 1970, Colvin R De Silva was appointed minister of Plantations, Industries and Constitutional Affairs and was asked to draft a new constitution, he consulted FP members on minority issues. But, as the FP supported the right-wing UNP, the members refused to cooperate. Instead SJV Chelvanayagam declared: "only God can save the Tamils".

The FP's right-wing opportunism was inexcusable. Having collaborated with the UNP and achieved nothing, its refusal to support the demands of the Tamils for a new constitution was indefensible. FP leaders clearly put their own political agenda above people's rights. Their propaganda about the Colombo government kept them alive among the people. Just like their Sinhala nationalist counterparts, the FP leaders spread nationalist propaganda to win mass support. Some claimed that, because the FP was taking a firm stand for a separate Tamil state, it was thus a principled stand. This was not the case. The FP joined the government when the FP's political leaders were assured of getting enough positions. The FP was busy organising 'Hindu' ladies meetings, etc. When, under pressure, the FP eventually agreed to participate in the discussion, none of the leaders showed any signs of making a serious effort.

The government of 1970 was progressive compared to the previous UNP governments. NM Perera, as finance minister, implemented some populist measures. Nationalisation, prioritising the development of local industry, and government subsidies for the small farmers and small scale businesses were some of its initiatives that significantly improved living conditions for workers and the poor. Each time JR Jayewardene had been finance minister, and he had been finance minister a few times, he had brought the country to its knees and made it dependent on foreign aid. Under NM Perera manufacturing boomed.

When a constituent assembly was established in 1971, the FP reluctantly supported it, as did all other political parties. Under the new constitution, the country was renamed the Republic of Sri

Lanka. The FP objected to this and later withdrew from the Assembly. The FP's withdrawal was considered a victory for the FP's youth wing which had begun to feel frustrated with their leaders.

Students were playing an increasingly important role in organising the masses. Eelam Tamilar Ilanjar Iyakkam, the Tamil Youth Movement, organised around 1970, was beginning to provide leadership. The League opposed the upper class/caste viewpoint of the FP leadership. Inspired by the Cuban revolution and various events of that time, a determined group of youth took control of the League. They did not, however, have the experience or understanding that their Sinhala counterparts had.

The introduction of Sinhala names in the late 1960s and 70s further fuelled the anger of youth. The introduction of words such as 'laksala' and 'salusala' were opposed by them. The names of corporation and various other government offices were also beginning to be changed. At this stage key leaders in the Tamil Youth League began to take up a new direction. Its leaders such as Sivakumar and Sathiaseelan began their vigorous propaganda for an armed struggle.

This is mainly due to the fact that they developed antagonism against all political parties that existed at that time – but particularly against the FP. The FP was ridiculed as a party for getting teacher transfers and other bits and pieces from the southern government. The FP's coalition with UNP also was massively unpopular. Almost all the negotiations the FP engaged in with the southern government had ended in failure. All this experience played a role in developing an anti-party mood among youth who were beginning to argue that they needed a 'new' way of struggle – ie armed struggle against the Sinhala state. Added to this combustible material was the introduction of new discriminative measures against Tamil students.

The government introduced a new selection method for the universities according to which Tamil students were asked to obtain higher marks in the Advanced Level exams in order to enter universities. This played a decisive role in forcing the students and youth to enter into a bitter struggle against the state.

A boycott on 22 May 1972, when the constitution was officially introduced, was the first major action by the Student League. The hartal was successful. In Jaffna, the new constitution was, almost literally, set on fire by the youth. A bomb was thrown into government buildings.

But the new constitution was a leap forward in terms of democratic rights. However, the advances it contained did not change anything for the minorities. Bearing in mind the riots of 1958, the LSSP leaders argued that the damage done to the Tamil minorities was of such an order that, to recover their trust, special concessions had to be made. However, the LSSP declared that, under the new constitution, the problems of the minority were solved. A United Front attempt to nationalise the press had a negative impact. Another disastrous policy of the United Front government was the introduction of a quota system for university entrance.

Policy of standardisation

With few factory or other opportunities for employment in the north or east of the Island, the government was the largest employer of labour in the area. Much of the employment it offered required university qualifications. Thus education became the most important factor in improving lives in the north and east. Until the late 1960s, the majority of university students were either from Colombo or Jaffna, mostly from privileged backgrounds. In particular, the developing capitalist class in Jaffna relied heavily on education as a means of retaining their wealth and status. With a high standard of schooling and numerous tuition centres, large numbers of candidates gained admission to universities around the country. In the north, students who performed well obtained admission to the few famous schools where they received a rigorous education.

In the north and east, including the areas in which the majority of people were poor, students did not have the same standards or facilities as those available to Jaffna or Colombo students. Thus, the majority of these poor students lost out in the competition for good degrees and, subsequently, the best employment opportunities.

The same was true of students from oppressed castes and from the Hill Country plantations. In some places they did not even have schools. Nor did they have the money to travel to and attend schools or universities away from their homes.

What was needed to improve and level educational opportunities was investment in building new schools and universities in the poor areas and subsidies to assist poorer students to obtain an education. In the 1970s, Srimavo Bandaranaike's government abolished university entry by merit only and introduced a quota system.

According to the quota Tamil students were required to score more than 250 out of the 400 available points in four subjects to obtain admission to university. This was reduced to 229 points for the Sinhala students. Even when this crude discrimination was later modified, the general bias remained.

Under the new system, 70% of places were reserved for allocation to a pre-set numbers of students from the different revenue districts comprising each university's catchment area. This provision restricted the admission of students from Jaffna and Colombo to a mere 30%. Before the introduction of this quota system, over 50% of medical and engineering students were from these regions. A large number of well-educated scholars from the famous Jaffna schools were not able to obtain university places.

The government also introduced legislation to prevent students applying to Indian and UK universities. The impact of the legislation was most strongly felt among the Tamil community as the majority of applicants who gained entry to Sri Lankan universities were from Jaffna. In order to circumvent the quota system, many scholars from the under-developed areas moved to Jaffna where, when they had completed their schooling, they stood a better chance of gaining entrance to a university than had they remained at home. As a result of this practice, Tamil students' entry to university was more than halved and, subsequently, still further reduced. Even though the privileged students in western areas were affected by the system, there was a manifold increase in the number of Sinhala students entering universities.

The Sinhala nationalist forces had argued that Tamil students were favoured by the Tamil examiners and that was the reason why such a high percentage of Tamils entered universities. They maintained that Tamils were disproportionately represented in university and government posts. The introduction of a quota system by the Srimavo government was well supported by the nationalist forces but, in the north, particularly in Jaffna, it provoked an angry reaction among students. Students who were active in the Tamil Youth League began to vigorously campaign against the system of 'standardisation' in universities, as they saw it as part of the attack on the Tamil-speaking people in Sri Lanka.

Rise of the student movement

The first successful protest against the standardisation was organised by students from St Patrick's College in Jaffna. They marched from Muttai veli (an area near Jaffna fort and town) to Kacheri (the Government Servant's office). Following this major success, students began to agitate. Previously a number of young people were active in a student organisation called Eelath Thamilar Ilanjar Iyakkam (Eelam Tamils Youth Movement). One of the early campaigners for armed struggle, Ponnuthurai Sivakumaran, was the key leader of this small organisation. He was later joined by Sathiaseelan and many others. Sathiaseelan, who was in charge of a student magazine called 'Tamil youth', began to write political editorials calling for a rejection of all parties and the taking up of a new path. During the 1970 election period he wrote: "We must teach a lesson to 'great' leaders and 'commanders'". It was a direct attack on the leader of the Tamil Congress, GG Ponnambalam, and the key leader of the FP Amirthalingam. This magazine published educational articles for the school students which were sent – at times for free – to a number of advanced level students. Many students who could not afford tuition from the most popular teachers relied on this magazine. The political editorial was an additional feature, but helped Sathiaseelan and Sivakumar to spread their propaganda among the students.

Sensing the anger among students they began to discuss about organising a big student march. Sivakumar, Sathiaseelan, Muthukumarasamy, Thavarajah, Ariyaratnam and many others began to mobilise for it. They called all student leaders to meet and discuss. Two meetings were held in the famous Jaffna Malayan café. There was a unanimous agreement about their anger against the FP. They decided not to involve the FP in any of their preparations. The march was called in the name of a new organisation called Tamil Students League (Tamil Manavar Peravai, TMP).

The march organised by the TMP on 23 November 1970 was the first ever big student demo. Over 10,000 students participated. Out of this TMP become a well-known organisation. The march started from Kokuvil Hindu college and ended in Muthai veli where a rally was held. Students demanded the resignation of the education minister and put forward slogans such as 'don't discriminate against us', 'are you discriminating against us because we are minorities', 'don't provoke racism', 'Why 229 for Sinhala students and 250 for Tamil students', etc.

The FP and others attempted to capture support. When members of the Communist Party (Maoist, also called the Ceylon Communist Party (Peking Wing)) joined the march as it was passing their office, students expressed anger and asked them to leave. This left group, known for its violent tactics, had made no attempt to campaign with the students. They offered no perspective for the developing situation. Their position on the national question on the other hand was almost the same as the JVP. While they argued for a united working class struggle, they ignored the nationalist mood that was developing among the Tamil students. They did not propose any organisational tactics for the campaign. But they intervened at times, as in this demo, to provoke violent clashes. They argued with the students that they should confront the police to achieve a 'concrete outcome' and that otherwise it will be 'just a march'.

But the students leading the march understood that confrontation with the police would be counterproductive and lead to the arrest of all the key students leaders and activists – eventually crippling the movement they were planning to build. They successfully resisted the Maoists and eventually made them leave the demo.

To date the Maoists have not changed their tactics, in general. Though they opportunistically later lent their support to what they claimed was a 'freedom struggle' they never put forward any perspective for that struggle. Their leader Sanmugathasan even boasted that they were a catalyst in propagating a violent response from the students. In his autobiography later written in exile he admits that they failed to organise the students. But he ignorantly took comfort with the claim that the youth who later took up the armed struggle had accepted 'Marxist-Leninist' politics. The Maoists' failure to measure the conditions developing around them, and their opportunist turn later toward Tamil nationalism destroyed this party.

Similarly the FP attempted to take pole position at the student rally. Amirthalingam stood behind the stage and insisted that he speak. Navaratnam also insisted that he should speak on behalf of his party. They gathered the students who supported them to put forward their case. However they were resisted by the student leaders such as Sathiaseelan who led the march and become the leader of the TMP later. Energised by this demo Sathiaseelan and others travelled to various parts of the North and East to win support. In their propaganda they argued for an armed struggle. A number of young people who participated in the TMP later joined or started the armed militant groups. V Prabhakaran, the leader of the Liberation Tigers of Tamil Eelam (LTTE) also came from the TMP.

Students, such as Sivakumar, who were determined that the next step should be an armed struggle, began their clandestine work. He was responsible for first violent act by the students. He bombed the car of the Deputy Minister Somaweera Chandrasiri during his visit to Jaffna to open a science department in Urumpirai Tamil junior school in 1971. Soon after, Sivakumar and Sathiaseelan bombed the Jaffna mayor Alfred Duraiyappa's car. Duraiyappa was later killed by Prabhakaran in 1975. Duraiyappa was a member of the SLFP – massive hatred was growing among the students at that time for the SLFP. Throughout 1972 and in the following years the SLFP office and their supporters were constantly attacked by the militants in protest at the SLFP-led new constitution. On 4 June 1972, the SLFP supporter and Nallur village council chairman, Kumarakulasingham, was shot and injured.

The TMP was wound up in 1973 with the arrest of a number of its leaders, including Sathiaseelan. Those active in the TMP were split into various formations. One section of them joined the FP leaders. Others formed the Tamil Elaingyar Peravai (TYL - Tamil Youth League) in 1973. Many militant organisations emerged from this.

Sivakumar who was arrested in 1970, on the day he bombed Santhirasiri's car, was released a few months later. He went into hiding from that time onwards to avoid capture by the police. However his luck did not last long. When he was surrounded by the police in 1974 he killed himself by swallowing cyanide. He became the first person to die by this method which was later used by the LTTE to prevent capture by the military. He was just 24 years old. His funeral was attended by all the key Tamil politicians and he became a sort of icon for building support for the armed struggle.

The growth of Tamil militancy

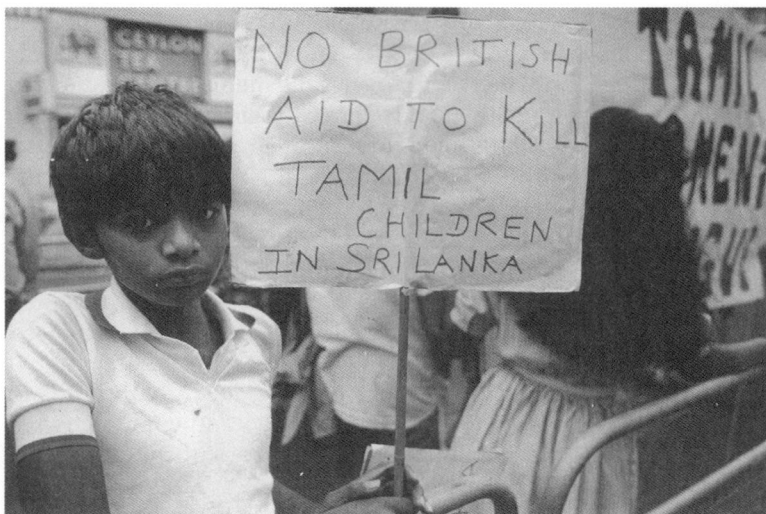

Protest in London in the 1980s

On 26 March 1971 the East Pakistan war of independence broke out. In December, India intervened and Bangladesh emerged as a sovereign country. The outcome of the Bangladeshi struggle gave the Tamil youth a massive boost in their struggle for equity with their Sinhala counterparts and they too, looked to India to aid their struggle. In February 1971 the FP leaders, having observed how India helped create Bangladesh, went to Tamil Nadu to seek help. By now DMK, which came to power in Tamil Nadu in 1967, was established as a strong force. The DMK leaders had a great deal of sympathy for the Sri Lankan Tamils. Karunanithi, one of the DMK leaders, met with the FP leaders and pledged his help.

Meanwhile, in India, the Indian Research and Analysis Wing (RAW), set up in the aftermath of the Indo-China war and modelled on the CIA in the US, began operations in all the countries of South Asia. The Indian central government considered the western influence, exercised through Pakistan a major threat. Some experts in India expressed the fear that their government's aid to the Sri Lankan Tamil separatist movement could revitalise the Dravidian separatist movement. However, the Indian ruling class had benefited from the creation of Bangladesh in that it had helped them further their regional interests. In the 1980s RAW began supporting Tamil militancy. This support boosted the confidence of the radicalised youth and undermined any political process that the FP leaders may have sought to pursue.

The gap between the young Tamils and the FP leaders was widening all the time. There was no existing medium in the country through which the youth could express their anger. In the late 1970s and in the early 1980s the name 'Tigers' began to become a household name. It represented all the youth who rebelled against the state and the Tamil leadership. Although as far back as 1961, an attempt to adopt that name had been made by some of the youth involved in FP activities, it was only in the mid-1980s that the word began to be exclusively associated with the liberation struggle and the Liberation Tigers of Tamil Eelam (LTTE) became a recognised organisation.

In the late 1960s, two names, Thangathurai and Kuttimani, emerged as a pole of attraction for radicalised young people who were seeking an alternative way to fight back. In 1969, students, including S Pushparaja, established the Tamil Liberation Organisation (TLO). Pushparaja's book 'My witness in Eelam struggle' (only available in Tamil) is an important read for scholars of this period. Pushparaja also claims that they were influenced by the Palestine Liberation Organisation (PLO). TLO sought to popularise liberation ideology. However TLO also suffered a setback after the arrest of almost all its leaders after a sloppy robbery of Puloli bank to fund their operations. When the TLO became dysfunctional the name was then allegedly taken by Kuttimani and Thangathurai, who renamed it TELO (Tamil Eelam Liberation Organisation). Many among the youth, including Prabhakaran, were drawn to them.

In the north, the methods of Kuttimani and Thangathurai did not appeal to the Tamil elite who regarded them as robbers. However the media and government attempts to vilify them as robbers did not hold water as the same accusation was levelled against anyone who raised a voice against the state. As these campaigns were the main form of resistance that existed, they won significant mass support. Out of a split in the TELO came various organisations, including the LTTE.

From the early 1970s, armed struggle became the key method of resistance against the Sri Lankan state. Following Sivakumar's death a massive wave of sympathy for the 'boys', as they were known, spread and countered the elite's attacks.

Although certain class divisions existed among the Tamil youth, a number of them began to unite behind the demand for a separate nation. A significant section of the educated upper-caste youth, who worked with the FP, decided that the FP leadership was too uncritical of the government leaders, and took a more radical stance. In turn, the FP leaders did not understand the mounting anger and frustration of the youth and continued their 'talks' with the government. Having more in common with the Sinhala capitalist class than with the struggling masses, the FP dismissed the young people's demands as 'unpractical'. In turn, the frustrated youth, considering that these leaders were sabotaging the demand for separatism, began to organise militant wings and violent attacks.

Police attack university, 12 November 1976

Tamil leaders turn towards separate state

On 2 October 1972, under mounting pressure from below, the FP leader SJV Chelvanayakam, resigned. When he returned to the north, the youth organised a massive welcome for him. At a mass meeting of thousands, Pushparaja cut his own hand and with his blood put pottu (forehead decoration) on the FP leader. This form of anointment became a tradition at FP meetings. Chelvanayakam declared that the FP was against the new constitution and demanded that the government hold a byelection as a test of support among the Tamils for the government reforms.

The FP leadership responded to the radicalisation among the youth by moving even further to the right. Having pretended to support the boys' call for a boycott of the 1972 constitution, the FP later, in order to enter parliament, took the oath of allegiance to the government. When Srimavo came to open Jaffna University in 1974, small bombs were planted by the youth throughout Jaffna.

Meanwhile the Communist Party's leading member was her interpreter and the CP as a whole, welcomed her. As Jaffna University could be used to divide the north and east, a division welcomed by the Jaffna elite, the youth wanted a University at Trincomalee.

The Srimavo government refused to call a byelection immediately, fearing outright victory for the FP leader. It took another three years, that is until 1975, before a byelection was called. Chelvanayakam's impressive victory in that election was seen as a triumph for the youth who had put all their energy into proving that the people preferred separation.

The youth, with a Tamil land and nation as their goal, sought separation and urged the FP to unite in fighting for this goal. They wanted the FP to demand a separate land for Tamils. Some FP leaders openly sought the same goal. One among them, A Rajaratnam, had played a role in setting up the 'Puli padai' (Tiger Army). But it was not until 1970, when militant activities among the youth increased, that they were able to muster the support of the FP leaders.

As we saw earlier, as early as 1972, Velupillai Prabhakaran and a few other young people had decided that armed struggle was the only way forward. Taking inspiration from events such as the 1971 JVP insurrection, they formed the Tamil New Tigers (TNT), a militant organisation committed to armed struggle for a separate Tamil country. However, initially, the TNT were only a tiny minority. Then, on 17 September 1972 Prabhakaran launched an attack on the Jaffna mayor Alfred Duraiappah. Although the attack was seen by the media as a personal revenge, Prabhakaran became a hero to the students. Some students perceived his method as the only way to make the FP leaders and the government listen to them. The government arrested numerous leading youth.

The FP leadership was confused about what stand it should take. To retain the allegiance of the masses they needed the support of the youth. To gain and keep that support, they gave rabblerousing speeches and organised protests. But they failed to formulate a coherent programme or strategy or, even, to take a strong stand in parliament against the parliamentary communal forces. They failed, too, to identify the friendly forces in the south. In all, they treated the situation as a game of 'clever politics'. In doing so, they calculated, wrongly, that, in the same way as JR Jayewardene had used Sinhala communalists in the south, they could use the radical youth to achieve their political goals.

Over the next few years, probably with some assistance from the Indian government, several student organisations were established including some armed units such as TELO. By 1976 the call for a united struggle of Tamils against the 'Sinhala nationalist state' was loud and clear.

Meanwhile in the south, the government was losing the support of the workers. To regain it, the UNP once more adopted communal tactics. The UNP, under JR Jayewardene who, since the death of Dudley Senanayake was its unchallenged leader, began to organise Satyagraghas and protests along communal lines. The economic difficulties the United Front government faced lead it to take drastic measures. Without proper planning, it introduced a rigorous rationing system. To this day, people remember the long bread queues of that period. To capitalise on the situation, the UNP promised that it would, if it won the next election, get rid of the queues. It was Jayewardene who directed the party machine in a series of marches on Buddhist temples and in the organisation of non-violent sit-ins. Having seen how brutally the government suppressed the JVP, he had learned not to make the mistake of setting violent rioters on minorities. At this stage, Sinhala nationalists within the SLFP wanted to take the party more to the right and started an assault against the left. There was a battle waged between right and left within the United Front.

It is important to note the role of the LSSP in these developments. It was the only force that was perceived as a non-Tamil party by many Tamils, but defended the rights of minorities. Its members fought the United Front's right wing on this issue. The Srimavo government, in order to undermine the principled stand of LSSP activists, employed tactics which were against the interest of the minorities. Despite intimidation, LSSP ministers refused to resign. Unable to oust them, the Srimavo government finally, in 1975, expelled the LSSP ministers. In protest against the United Front's extension of the government for another two years, as allowed in the new constitution, Jayewardene resigned.

The FP, pressured by the youth, adopted the demand for a separate nation rather than for federalism. Militant youth had attempted to either attack or, even, kill any MP who voted with the government. They had also threatened to attack anyone who opposed their demand for a separate country. On several occasions, V Prabhakaran stayed at FP president Amirthalingam's house, continuing to argue for the rejection of exclusively political means of struggle. At the FP's annual convention on 9 September 1973, Amirthalingam proposed the resolution that: "the only way open to the Tamil nation is to establish self-rule in their traditional homeland in the exercise of the inalienable right of every nation to self-determination".

The political heat had its own momentum. The youth wing was strengthening fast and even the right-wing youth who stood with the FP leaders became more restless. There is evidence that these young people were competing among themselves for power and control of events.

After Chelvanayakam's resignation, the FP gave into the youth's demands and the campaign for separation intensified. The Party adopted the rhetoric of the Dravidian movement in Tamil Nadu. In January 1974 the Tamil Nadu government helped organise the fourth World Tamil Research Conference in Jaffna. What started as a minor incident with the police at the conference – mild intimidation of some participants – turned into a horrific attack against those present. Nine people died and at least 50 were injured.

In 1975, a byelection was held which the FP won by a considerable margin. The win gave the youth of the Party a huge boost as they saw it as victory for their stand on separation. The LSSP, unable to work out the political direction that the youth who were joining the FP were likely to take, had collaborated with the CP in putting up a candidate for the byelection. Some left-leaning students had supported the CP candidate who managed to win a respectable vote. Despite their support for socialist ideas the youth wing continued to oppose the LSSP and CP candidates who they saw as collaborators of the SLFP. Their campaign to force the FP to take a firm stand for separation had won support when, in 1976, a significant change had taken place. All the Tamil parties had come together to form the Tamil United Liberation Front (TULF, previously formed as TUF in 1972). At their first national convention held in Vaddukoddai on 1 May 1976, they adopted the famous Vaddukoddai Resolution. The resolution was heavily influenced by Sheikh Mujibur Rahman's agreement with India during the struggle for independence of Bangladesh.

Now almost all the Tamil organisations claim that their strategy is based on the Vaddukoddai Resolution (VKR). It is worth looking at some details of the resolution for that reason. Those who claim this should elaborate in what way they are planning to fight and what are their perspectives, strategy, aims, etc.

Summary of Vaddukoddai Resolution

Until its final section, the content of the Vaddukoddai Resolution (VKR) mainly focuses on the history of Sri Lanka, starting with the pre-colonial period.

It describes briefly the fight for Tamil rights and the continued repressive nature of Sri Lankan governments since independence, highlighting the pogroms against Tamils. Next, it criticises the Constituent Assembly of 1972 and its failure to pay attention to the aspiration of the Tamil masses. Finally it outlines its demands and calls on all, particularly the youth, to fight for them. This final section is the most important part of the resolution.

Language of the resolution

Despite calling for a 'socialist Tamil Eelam', the resolution fails to deal with, or even mention, the class nature of society. Also, there are a number of mistakes in its brief history due, most probably, to misinterpretation of history by the upper class.

The first point to note is that it was the Tamil youth, students and workers along with their Sinhala and Muslim counterparts, and not their self-appointed leaders, who played the key role in the movement for independence.

Terms such as 'Sinhala nation' and 'Tamil nation' are used which are incorrect. The 'nation state' as a modern concept did not exist before the rise of capitalism. Tamil Eelam is a modern name which refers to the areas where mainly Tamils lived in Lanka. Prior to the colonial period these areas were divided into a number of autonomous regions and at no time in history did a concentration of people exist as a consolidated nation called 'Tamil Eelam' or, even, 'Eelam'.

The question of rights is more important than the question of who was the first to come to the island. It is oppression that has to be fought. The Tamil-speaking people including the masses, the plantation workers and the rest of the poor, are entitled to all democratic rights including the right to self-determination. When terms such as 'Tamil nation' or 'Sinhala nation' are used it is generally misleading and, at times, communal or even racist. The Sinhala communalists often use the term 'Sinhala nation' as if denoting 'Sinhala superiority' in relation to the rest of the population. Tamil nationalism which, to some extent, developed as a counterpart to Sinhala nationalism, also copied the phraseology of the Sinhala chauvinists. This copying can be seen in some of the terminology in the documents prepared by the Tamil elite in the 1970s and which set the trend for the 'Tamil nationalist phraseology'. Significant sections of the VKR display this error.

Fighting against oppression does not require the oppressed to copy the language of their oppressors. Statements such as: "Sinhalese people have used their political power to the detriment of the Tamils" do not further the aspirations of the Tamils to end all oppression. There is a need to differentiate between the Sinhala people and the Sinhala state.

Since independence in Sri Lanka a significant number of Sinhala workers and poor people have supported the rights of the Tamil people. Their continued support and unity with the Tamil people is crucial to challenge the oppressors. It is the wealthy Sinhala elite which has used ethnic differences and nationalist propaganda to rally mass support and maintain their power and dominance. It is they who organised mobs and were responsible for the pogroms against the Tamil-speaking people. The Tamil-speaking people, as a consequence of the growth of Sinhala nationalism, have suffered severely. But the Sinhala masses have also lost out.

The defeat of the Tamil people has not improved the lot of the overwhelming majority of Sinhala people – the working class and poor masses. It was only in 1983, after success in defeating the workers' movement, that JR Jayewardene, a pro-capitalist and chauvinist politician, was able to carry out the horrific pogroms against the Tamil-speaking people. The blame lies with the ruling elite, not with the oppressed Sinhala working class. It is necessary to make this distinction now to counter the continuing onslaught of Sinhala Buddhist nationalist propaganda.

VKR and the 1972 constitution

The VKR's critique of the 1972 constitution has its pluses and minuses. On the minus side it reflects the political position of the leadership of the TULF rather than the interests of ordinary Tamils.

Despite their Tamil nationalist rhetoric, the FP leaders, prior to the passing of the resolution, were concerned about the youth's increasing domination of the movement.

To comprehend the extent and nature of this domination, it is important to set it in the context of the period: the 1960s and 1970s, decades of radical upheaval and revolution throughout the world. Nearly all the movements were, to a greater or lesser extent, radical left-wing or socialist movements. In Sri Lanka, the youth's stand constituted a threat to the Sinhala ruling class as well as to the Tamil leaders of the FP.

In 1965, SJV Chelvanayakam was prepared to reach a compromise with the UNP – to enter a marriage of convenience. In contrast, the FP leadership, in its own political interests rather than in those of the Tamils, ignored the SLFP. It did so despite the fact that SLFP government had accepted all the points requested by the FP in the agreement and promised to implement them. At this stage, the LSSP, regardless of its decision to work with the SLFP, stood for more far-reaching rights, in a socio-economic sense, than the FP.

The 1972 constitution did not reflect the aspirations of the Tamil masses and the opportunity for national unity was missed. All the parties, including the LSSP, lost the trust of the Tamil-speaking masses. The TULF, while collaborating against the interests of the Tamil-speaking masses, also tried to exploit the situation to strengthen itself, also failed. It too had underestimated the level of anger among the youth. So its claim that it 'tried and failed' is not credible.

Declaration of the resolution

The final section of the resolution is the most important section. It is quite easy to understand why the right-wing TULF leaders did not contribute to it. Although it reflects confusion as to what class society and the 'right to self-determination' actually mean, its demand for a secular socialist state, makes it a powerful resolution. Importantly, it states that observance of caste will be punishable by law. It was no secret then that most of the TULF leaders did not agree with the conclusion that read:

"This convention resolves that restoration and reconstitution of the Free, Sovereign, Secular, Socialist State of Tamil Eelam, based on the right of self-determination inherent to every nation, has become inevitable in order to safeguard the very existence of the Tamil Nation in this Country."

Furthermore the VKR declared that economic "development shall be on the basis of socialist planning and there shall be a ceiling on the total wealth that any individual or family may acquire." This bold declaration reflected the mood of the youth quite accurately. However it also shows the confusion that existed in the understanding of the right to self-determination.

All the parties involved, except the Ceylon's Workers Congress, the trade union of the plantation workers, agreed on the points made in the VKR. The reason for the plantation workers' disagreement was because the majority of them lived outside the territories defined by the VKR. Their disagreement was registered by the convention.

In summary, VKR consists of the following points:

1. Full and equal rights to all of citizenship in the state of Tamil Eelam;
2. The adoption of democratic decentralisation;
3. Caste system to be eradicated;
4. The State to be a secular state;
5. Tamil to be a national language on a par with the Sinhala language;
6. The final point declared:

"That Tamil Eelam shall be a Socialist State wherein the exploitation of man by man shall be forbidden, the dignity of labour shall be recognised, the means of production and distribution shall be subject to public ownership and control while permitting private enterprise in these branches within limit prescribed by law, economic development shall be on the basis of socialist planning and there shall be a ceiling on the total wealth that any individual or family may acquire."

This declaration was the bravest and most advanced declaration to come from the Tamils since the early days of the struggle for independence. To demand a socialist state, with full and equal rights for all citizens and the eradication of the caste system was a formidable step forward.

However no member of the FP leadership supported the Resolution. Hence no attempt whatsoever was made to work out a programme or strategy to fight for these ideas. The leadership had no idea of what socialism meant or what becoming a 'socialist state' involved. They were interested only in the formation of a 'separate Tamil Eelam' and saw themselves as the future leaders of that separate state. It is said that when, in 1986, TULF leader Amirthalingam was asked: "When you passed the Vaddukoddai resolution, what were your plans about how you were going to achieve Tamil Eelam?" he replied: "Thamby, whoever thought about all that at that time!" This response demonstrates the attitude of the FP/TULF leaders.

The 'boys' set out to prepare what they believed to be 'socialist programmes' for their groups. In 1976 the LTTE was formed. Its manifesto, published in 1978, was translated into many languages and made an appeal to youth movements around the world. It bore a remarkable resemblance to the VKR. It stated:

"Our fundamental objectives are:

• Total independence of Tamil Eelam. The establishment of a sovereign, socialist democratic people's government

• Abolition of all forms of exploitation of man by man and the establishment of a socialist mode of production ensuring that the means of production and exchange of our country becomes the ownership of our people."

The document set out the following strategy for the LTTE:

"The Liberation Tigers of Tamil Eelam has resolved to work in solidarity with the world national liberation movements, socialist states, international working class parties. We uphold an anti-imperialist policy and therefore, we pledge our militant solidarity with the oppressed humankind in the Third World in their struggle against imperialism, neo-colonialists, Zionism, racism and other forces of reaction."

The document demonstrates some of the confusion that existed at that time. The resolutions were based on a superficial understanding of the polarisation occurring in international relations. For example, it treated Russia, China and Cuba as all being, simply, 'socialist states', failing to recognise the radical differences among them.

This was the period of revolutionary tendencies among Tamils. The LTTE was one of many groups but, in the 1980s, it emerged as the dominant group.

By now, most of the Tamil members of the LSSP were leaving it. They had lost faith in the Party because many of its leaders were participating in the coalition government.

Reportedly, within a year of signing the VKR and agreeing to the demand for a socialist Tamil Eelam, the FP leaders made a secret pact with the right-wing capitalist and communalist UNP leader, JR Jayewardene. Later, JR Jayewardene used the agreement to persuade the CWC leader, Thondaman to agree to his proposals.

Last stand of TULF and concretisation of division

In the 1977 elections, the 'boys' campaigned for the new Tamil United Liberation Front (TULF) alliance. Their election manifesto, which called for "Tamil Eelam: the right to self-determination", was not written in the spirit of the VKR's final demands. After the deaths of GG Ponnampalam, M Thiruchelvam and SJV Chelvanayakam, the leadership of the TULF passed into the hands of Amirthalingam, a right-wing member of the Front who had lost his parliamentary seat in the 1970 election. Amirthalingam supported the 'boys' activities. By pushing for the development of a separatist ideology within the TULF, he sought to establish personal dominance of the Front. Under his leadership, the Front's election manifesto combined an attack on minority rights with hatred against Sinhala people.

During the election campaign, both Mr and Mrs Amirthalingam spoke at meetings in numerous places and made aggressive and insulting remarks to the Sinhala masses as distinct from the Sinhala leadership or government. Many of the young people who attended these meetings remember how Mrs Amirthalingam promised that, should they be elected, she would rip the skin off the Sinhala people and wear it as slippers. As a result of attending these meetings, a number of Tamil youths were recruited to the militant organisations but were not given any education whatsoever about the history of Sri Lanka, nor the origin of the ethnic conflict.

Right-wing propaganda claimed that the Sinhala people had always been racist towards Tamils. No attempt was made to explain how it had come about that the Sinhala masses were standing shoulder to shoulder with Tamil masses to defend the rights of minorities. No mention was made of the fact that the Sinhala ruling class, to come to and hold on to power, had systematically used ethnic division. No indication was given that all was to worsen under the JR Jayewardene regime. It was a monstrous mistake not to warn the Tamil masses of the dangers of the UNP government. Instead the

Tamil elite collaborated with the UNP!

TULF education was imprinted in the minds of many cadres of the movements that spread in the 1980s. The TULF election manifesto adopted the VKR in principle. One section of the manifesto was entitled: "Liberation - how will it be achieved?" The answer given was:

"The Tamil nation must take the decision to establish its sovereignty in its homeland on the basis of its right to self-determination. The only way to announce this decision to the Sinhalese government and to the world is to vote for the Tamil United Liberation Front. The Tamil-speaking representative who get elected through these votes, while being members of the National State Assembly of Ceylon, will also form themselves into the 'National Assembly of Tamil Eelam' which will draft a constitution for the State of Tamil Eelam and to establish the independence of Tamil Eelam by bringing that constitution into operation either by peaceful means or by direct action or struggle"!

The manifesto also stated:

"Hence, the Tamil United Liberation Front seeks in the general election the mandate of the Tamil nation to establish an independent sovereign, secular, socialist state of Tamil Eelam that includes all the geographically continuous areas that have been the traditional homelands of the Tamil-speaking people in this country."

The 'boys' and the people were soon to discover what monstrous deceits these claims were. The 1977 election result was a decisive statement of what was to come.

The SLFP suffered a major defeat and only managed to retain eight seats. The UNP won 140 seats with 50.9% of the vote. TULF won a landslide in the Tamil areas with 18 seats and became the main opposition party, the first Tamil party to do so. The LSSP, having managed a major victory in the previous election, lost more than half its vote and all its seats and was never to recover from this defeat. The workers and poor never forgave them for their cross-class approach. A section of the LSSP, under Siritunga Jayasuriya, Vickramabahu Karunararna, Vasudeva Nanayakara, split away and formed the Nava Sama Samaja Party (NSSP). Originally, the NSSP took an improved stand on the national question and had the support of a considerable number of workers and poor. Members within the NSSP, led by Siritunga Jayasuriya, who had previously opposed the LSSP's participation in a cross-class coalition, now argued for a united struggle of the masses and stood for the right to self-determination, including that of separation, of the Tamil-speaking people.

Even after the overwhelming support for struggle shown by the Tamil masses, reflected in the election results, the TULF wavered. As a leader of the opposition A Amirthalingam was ineffective. He had, in fact, opted to work with the government. While the TULF leaders were negotiating with the UNP government for ministerial positions, a minority in the NSSP was promoting the right to Tamil self-determination. What stood between the NSSP and the Tamil youth was the right-wing leadership of the TULF which systematically prevented a united struggle. The TULF leadership thrived on the Tamil/Sinhala divide on the issue of sharing power with right-wing Sinhala leaders.

But, as JR Jayewardene began to show his true colours, the TULF leadership was forced to distance itself from the UNP. The election was to prove a disaster for the great majority of the Sri Lankan people. Jayewardene set about reforming the constitution and establishing a semi-dictatorial executive presidency. He adopted neoliberal policies, and began the process of privatising national services. An early victim was the Ceylon Transport Board. Claiming that it was running at a loss, transport properties and services were sold off at prices well below their value.

Jayewardene also unleashed the communalist 'lumpens'. Within a month of the elections, an organised gang attacked Tamils in the south. The government claimed that the attack was spontaneous, that is, random and unpredicted, but there is irrefutable evidence that they were planned and carried out by very well-organised gangs. For more than a week, the government failed to take action to stop the attacks. When JR Jayewardene was questioned in parliament by A Amirthalingam, he delivered his famous reply:

"People become restive when they hear that a separate state is to be formed. Whatever it is, when statements of that type are made, the newspapers carry them throughout the island, and when you say that you are not violent, but that violence may be used in time to come, what do you think the other people in Sri Lanka will do? How will they react? If you want to fight, let there be a fight; if it is peace, let there be peace; that is what they will say. It is not what I am saying. The people of Sri Lanka say that."

The sentence: "If you want to fight, let there be a fight; if it is peace, let there be peace" was published in all the Tamil media. "If you want war we will give you war," is still well remembered by that particular generation. JR Jayewardene was manipulating public opinion when he said: "that is what they will say. It is not what I am saying. The people of Sri Lanka say that." His statement was an example of the way in which the Sinhala nationalist right-wing rulers justified their attacks. The implication that there were people in Sri Lanka who wanted war was a complete distortion. The Tamil masses never wanted war. All they wanted was their rights. Similarly the Sinhala masses wanted better living conditions and respect for their rights. It was only the ruling elite who benefitted from unrest.

Having obtained an unexpected outright majority in the parliamentary elections, the prime minister sought to dispense with the TULF and refused to give them the five district ministerial seats he had promised them. Instead a Tamil UNP member was chosen.

A TULF leader who had crossed over to the UNP was also made a minister. A Amirthalingam publicly accused him of being a traitor and soon after, he was murdered by militants. It soon became clear that JR Jayewardene was determined to increase his attacks on Tamil rights. However, to change the constitution which established the executive presidency, he needed the TULF's support. The TULF gave him their support and JR Jayewardene became the first executive president of Sri Lanka. However, despite intimidation by UNP-organised gangs, his attacks on workers' rights did not go unchallenged.

Among younger TULF members, anger was mounting against its leaders. The VKR and all the revolutionary promises during the election had come to nothing and there was no sign of firm action from the TULF leaders. A book entitled 'Towards the socialist Tamil Eelam' by Anton Balasingam was published and widely read. Balasingam, who was living in London at that time, was later to become the LTTE's chief advisor. Radicalised youth were travelling to Lebanon, Palestine, and other places for military training. A gap opened between the radicalised youth who wanted action and the TULF elite who, mixing in elite political circles, were locked in negotiations and the 'day to day political game'. Incredibly, when draconian laws, such as the Prevention of Terrorism Act, were moved, the TULF did not attend parliament to oppose them. It was the Left who voted against them and who organised protest meetings outside Parliament.

Last stand of the old workers' movement

JR Jayewardene, second from left, inagurating a container depot, 1 August1980

As a result of the disastrous economic policies of JR Jayewardene, unemployment soared, wages shrank and inflation increased. Farmers and small traders suffered under the 'open' economy. Once again, under the leadership of the NSSP and the LSSP, which retained some control of the unions, workers were organised. Jayewardene was waiting for a head-on collision with the workers. He had learned a great deal during Srimavo's brutal suppression of the JVP. With increased investment in defence and with organised mobs behind him he began his attack on workers' rights and conditions.

In many ways the 1980s were a turning point in the history of Sri Lanka. The decade is known as a period of neoliberal offensives across the world. With right-wing ideologies and anti-working class programmes, US President Ronald Reagan and British Prime Minister Margaret Thatcher came to power. But it was, perhaps, in Sri Lanka that these policies were most stringently applied. Jayewardene opened the economy up for exploitation. He invited the IMF to advise the government and followed every step they dictated.

The UNP-led government began to amend labour legislation with the object of curtailing union rights. For example, the Public Service Act of 1979 effectively outlawed strikes in the government sector and essential services. Next, the UNP established a trade union which workers were, literally, forced to join. It became obvious that without a defensive struggle by the unions, it would not be possible to safeguard the rights that had been won over the years.

On 8 and 9 March 1980, the Joint Trade Union Action Committee (JTUAC) held a convention. The convention was a warning shot to Jayewardene. More than 4,000 trade unionists participated. The JTUAC sent its demands to the government, including a demand for a pay rise. To pressurise the government to accept its demands, the JTUAC called for a national protest and a half- day strike on 5 June.

Ratmalana railway workers at begining of strike, 1980

The JR Jayewardene-led government not only refused to accept the demands but also refused to enter into any negotiations with the JTUAC. A few days before the protest, Jayewardene addressed a meeting of the Jathika Sewaka Sangamaya (JSS), the UNP-controlled union. He asked them to organise a counter-protest and observe the day as a 'day of cooperation with government'.

On the day of the protest the JSS, with the blessing of the President, unleashed their violence against ordinary trade unionists and protesters. JSS thugs were transported by public transport buses (CTB), driven by UNP members or supporters. More than 40,000 workers went on strike. Cyril Mathew, the Minister for Industry was a real thug. He was allegedly involved in all the racist attacks against the Tamils in the south. His book, titled 'Sinhalese! Rise to Protect Buddhism', was circulated to recruit gang members. He moved his men to take control of the streets. The police played a passive role and let the violence carry on. Many trade unionists were attacked and Mr D Somapala, father of five young children and a well-known trade unionist, was killed.

The government refused to take any serious action against the violence it had provoked and refused to submit to any demands. Instead it continued to attack workers' rights. A month later the on 7 July a spontaneous strike erupted in the Ratmalana workshop where 12 railway workers had been dismissed two days earlier without reason. They were sacked on the charge that they tried to sabotage work on 5 June!

Workers at a general strike meeting in the auditorium in Colombo 28 July 1980

Management's refusal to negotiate with the outraged workers led to this spontaneous action. The strikers, while demanding the reinstatement of the dismissed workers, also raised the earlier demands for a pay rise (Rs300) that was put forward by the 5 June action. This forced the JTUAC to meet on 11 July and the meeting concluded by calling for a general strike on 18 July.

The government responded by introducing emergency rule two days before, on 16 July. JTUAC was banned from holding any public meeting from the day of the strike. But on the day the general strike began JR Jayewardene spoke at a public meeting of UNP supporters where he spelled out what his intentions. He stated that under his regulation any worker who struck would be deemed to have vacated his post. He declared that 'the workers who absented themselves on that day had vacated their posts, and that they need not report for work thereafter' This horrific, undemocratic and direct confrontation with the workers, attempting to deny the democratic right to strike, angered them even more. More unions joined the strike and it continued until 22 July.

The general strike had a big impact in the north. While a number of young people were involved in postering to promote the strike and mobilisation for it, TULF leaders took the side of JR Jayewardene.

Disgracefully, even the LSSP, whose support was in decline at this

Troops guard parliament buildings during the general strike and state of emergency, 8 August 1980

Government attempt to seize the GCSU HQ defeated by 4,000 strikers defending the building during the 1980 general strike

stage, refused to give their full backing as they thought the strike did not have political demands! The Communist Party had a similar position. The JVP was in total confusion and refused to give support. Others on the sectarian left keenly attacked other lefts but failed to act and lead the workers. The NSSP was the only left to throw itself into defending the strikers and work towards leading them politically. Some trade union leaders, despite being members of the CP or JVP, defied their party position to join the strike. Other lefts, apart from the NSSP, failed to understand the importance of the strike and the utmost urgency to defend it.

The UNP was determined to smash the workers' conditions. There was a rapid deterioration of living conditions and a widening of the ethnic gap. Jayewardene was waiting for an opportunity to use the Tamil/Sinhala divide to break the unions' strength and divide the community so he could implement neoliberal policies and strengthen his grip on the government.

Jayewardene was fanatical in wanting to use this spontaneous strike to break the backbone of the workers' movement once and for all. United action by all the trade unions and with the correct political leadership could have defeated the UNP government. However, the betrayal of the LSSP and the division that had already emerged among the left, combined with the brutal force of the

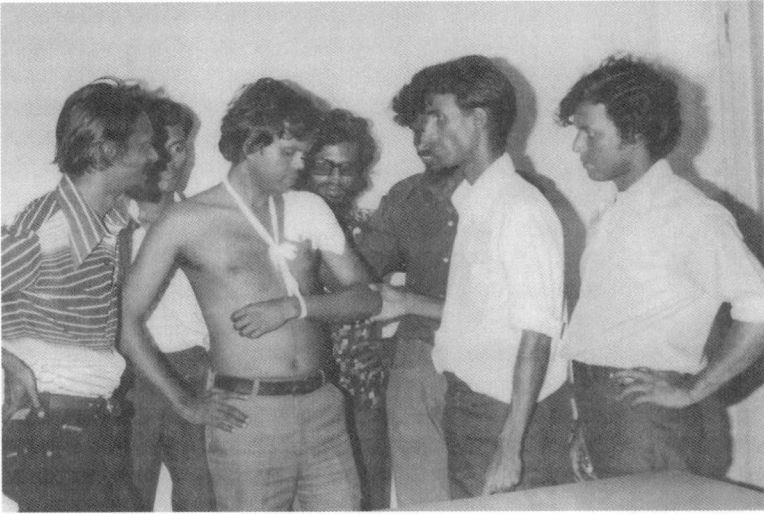

GCSU leader after release, 14 January 1980

government led to a vicious defeat of the strike, the scars of which remains to this date.

Workers who turned up to work on 21 and 22 July were told that they no longer had a job. They were locked out despite the huge disruption it caused to public services. In that month alone over 40,000 workers lost their jobs in this way. The number of jobs lost is estimated to be 80,000 to 100,000. Among those victimised were the leading trade unionists. Siritunga Jayasuriya, general secretary of the United Socialist Party (USP) then in the NSSP, gives the following account:

"The defeat experienced at the 1980 July general strike had a great impact upon the NSSP. The NSSP was the livewire of the July general strike. The UNP government led by JRJ sacked the employees to the score of 60,000, including UE Perera, S Sathyapala, Dharmabandu of the Railway, Nandasena, Mahinda Silva, Nimal Punchihewa of the Local Government Service, KJ Silva, Gerad Gamage of the government Office Service, JD Silva and LP Perera of the Teacher Service, Sawanadasa, Gunasena Mahanama and Pitigala of the Clerical Service, Quintus Liyanage, EAP Alwis, Reginald Fernando of the government Press, Regie, Bandusena, Premalal of the Ratmalana Railway Workshop, Sarath Wimalarathna of the People's Bank and many other trade union leaders and activists attached to the NSSP, under the draconian emergency laws of the JR government.

"The convenor of the Joint Trade Union Action Committee that gave leadership to this general strike was LW Panditha, who was also a Leader of the Communist Party. The Ceylon Mercantile Union and the Hospital Service union did not join the Strike; hypocritically citing all sorts of self-serving reasons, they abstained from supporting it. Although the JVP tried to prevent the Lanka Teachers' Union from joining the Strike, its leader HN Fernando courageously rejected the JVP scabs' demands, motivating the union to energetically join the strike. (HN Fernando is the brother-in-law of JVP founder Rohana Wijeweera). The JVP acted as strike-breaking scabs against the general strike. Comrade Somapala was murdered by gunshot in the brutal state terror launched against the strikers; Upathissa Gamanayake (a JVP leader), who turned up to pay a floral tribute to the dead body, could not reach the coffin as the workers gathered there grabbed him and threw that wreath of flowers into the Beira Lake. That very protest at Comrade Somapala's funeral showed the hatred of the working class towards the JVP for its stance of not supporting the strike.

"The general strike failed before the cruel state suppression of the UNP Government. Because all the trade unions affiliated to the NSSP had joined the strike, the defeat was felt vividly by it. The trade union leaders lost the organic contacts they had had with the working class. The political degeneration suffered by the NSSP at a latter stage was a poisoned fruit of the defeat of the 1980 July general strike. The Black July 1983 racist holocaust occurred within the prevailing context of 'strike defeat' nostalgia."

A large number of workers committed suicide due to the loss of their jobs. Many unions never recovered from this attack. The government sealed a number of trade union offices, took all their files, office equipment, etc. The Jayewardene regime did not stop even there. It went on the rampage against the democratic rights and other political parties and prevented trade union activities throughout his regime. With the workers' movement out of the way the UNP government went ahead with imposing a free market economy. Sri Lanka was the first country in the region to open up its economy for global exploitation.

A sign of the frustration of the defeat of the general strike was shown in the north when UNP leader R Balasundaram was shot dead by the militants at the end of 1980.

Burning of Jaffna Library

Jaffna library

Tamil militants supported the strike despite the TULF elite's disagreements. Many workers went on strike in the north and east. The TULF's degeneration become even more clear when Amirthalingam decided not to stand in the presidential election held in 1982, persuaded not to by Prime Minister Ranasinge Premedasa, another notorious leader of the UNP.

The government continued to provoke the militants with direct attacks. One of the major events that settled in the minds of militant youth at that time was the burning of Jaffna library on 2 June 1981. This library was considered to be one of the most important libraries in Asia with over 90,000 books. Government officials recently accepted that this was an organised act by the then government.

The attack on education had been one of the main recruitment agents for young people to the struggle. The burning of Jaffna library further strengthened this process.

1983 pogrom and beginning of civil war

On 23 July 1983 the LTTE ambushed a military truck and killed 13 soldiers. The UNP government reacted quickly to capitalise on this incident. Instead of following regular procedures, a mass funeral for the soldiers was planned in Colombo. UNP minister Cyril Mathew, with other right-wing members of the government, planned riots and attacks on the funeral day. A wealth of information has since emerged indicating how leading members of the UNP government played the leading role in organising the mobs. It appeared they had been waiting for such an 'opportunity' to present itself.

Sirisena Cooray, a leading UNP member, later pointed out that President JR Jayewardene had been completely aware of the situation. Cooray wrote: "This was madness. Like Mr Premadasa (then prime minister) I knew that all hell was likely to break loose when those bodies are brought to Colombo... If the president listened to Mr Premadasa, the 1983 July riots could have been avoided and the history of this country would have been different."

Cooray also pointed out that: "There was an organised crowd present, making a huge show of grief, weeping hysterically." Mr Premadasa himself later joined the gangs, not to miss out on the opportunity to gain control (or authority) among the communalists!

Jayewardene expressed the mindset of the communal thugs throughout his political career. Soon after his election victory he announced "I am not worried about the opinion of the Jaffna people now... Now we cannot think of them. Not about their lives or of their opinion about us... The more you put pressure in the north, the happier the Sinhala people will be here... really, if I starve the Tamils out, the Sinhala people will be happy..."

This, and his infamous declaration of war, had already given a massive boost to the communal forces. The UNP's brutal suppression of the general strike in 1980 was the key turning point that gave the Sinhala nationalists a commanding position within the government. Several acts of violence took place in the south against Tamils even before 1983. These were completely ignored by the government even after repeated requests for action.

On 24 July the bodies of the 13 soldiers were brought to Colombo. Organised mobs began to attack the Tamils in the south. Soon, the attacks spread to southern parts of the country. The government declared a curfew and the police and military were brought in. But the government forces were used as protection for the mobs rather than to protect the people from the mobs. Members of the mobs used government vehicles to move around. As reported in the media around the world, the mobs used electoral registers to identify Tamils and Tamil properties. (Even before the deaths of the 13 soldiers, 50 Tamils had been murdered and details of the murders had been published in the media). The communalists spread numerous rumours; one was that the LTTE was coming to the south to attack Sinhala people.

Between 400 and 3,000 people were killed in one day. More than 18,000 homes were damaged. More than 100 industrial plants and 20 garment factories were destroyed. Around 150,000 people lost their jobs and over 100,000 people became refugees. A day after the riots, 53 political prisoners were killed in prison. The killings took place in the notorious Welikada high security prison and sent a shock wave through the Tamil-speaking areas. All the political prisoners, including the LTTE members detained under the Prevention of Terrorism Law, were cruelly tortured and murdered. Some prisoners, who escaped this brutality and are now living in various parts of the world, explained how Sinhala prisoners helped Tamil prisoners escape the mob's attack. The government maintained that it was angry Sinhala prisoners who attacked and killed Tamil prisoners. This was a complete fabrication.

Demo in London with Dave Nellist, then socialist Labour MP, 30 July 1983

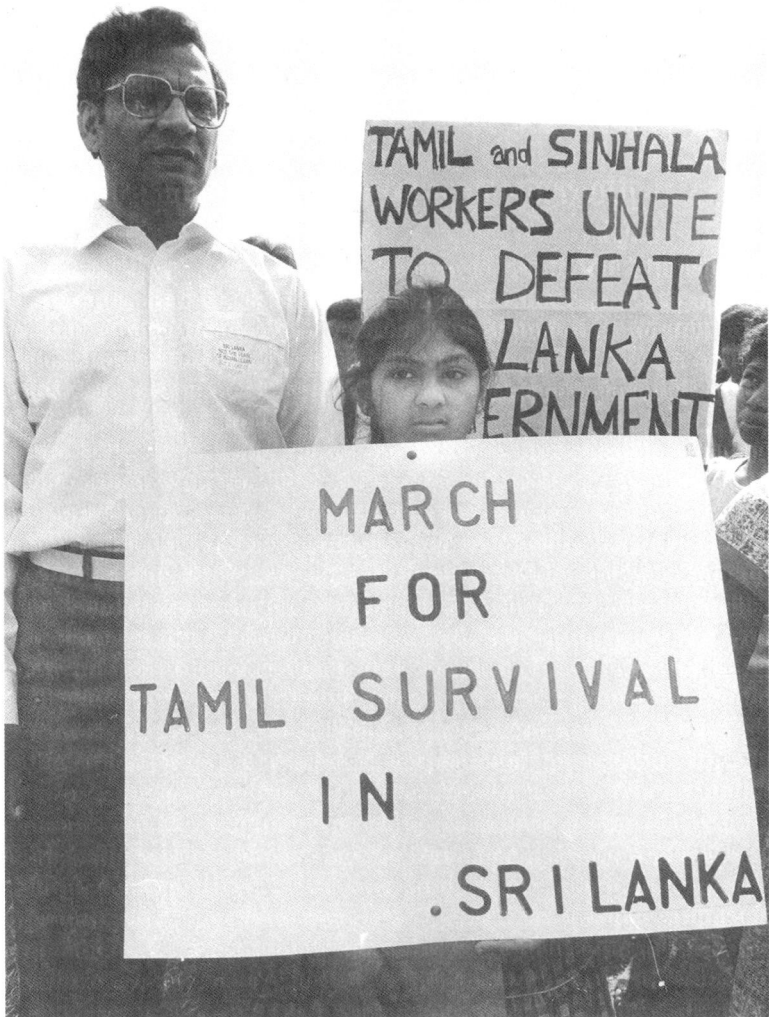

Demo in London, 30 July 1983

Throughout the south there were Sinhala people, including Siritunga Jayasuriya, then a leading member of the NSSP, now General Secretary of the United Socialist party, who tried to defend the Tamils from the attacks. They risked their own lives by hiding Tamil friends in their homes and defending them in the street. As a result, a number of Sinhala people were also assaulted.

With the attacks continuing, the President, retreating to the presidential palace, announced that: "the time has come to accede to the clamour and the national respect of the Sinhala people", a statement he repeated after the attacks. For the next four days, the President did not speak a word. When he did speak, he acknowledged that the attacks had been carried out by the Sinhala people and declared that it was time that the Sinhala people were given national respect.

The minister of state, Ananda Tissa de Alwis, acknowledging that the attacks had planned and executed by organised Sinhala mobs, went on to blame the left parties for planning them. However, the mentality of then government is summarised in the interview Jayewardene gave to New International in 1981. He declared:

"The political decisions I have taken may have been right or wrong but that doesn't matter. In my own behaviour, there is nothing to be ashamed of. I have done nothing mean. I know they say I am a strategist and a schemer but you cannot be a leader unless you scheme – not in politics or in war or in any human affair. Even a boxer has to scheme – and I was a boxer when I was young – you pretend to hit the face but you hit the stomach. Oh yes, you have to scheme."

While claiming to represent ordinary Sinhala people, JRJ organised attacks on minorities in order to maintain his position in power. Even

Demo in London 30 July 1983

right-wing historians, such as AJ Wilson who was in close contact with the UNP leadership at that time, agreed that "Jayewardene was out of control of the situation". He even advised the Tamil opposition leader, A Amirthalingam not to come to Colombo because he could "not guarantee his safety". The Tamil United Liberation Front (TULF) leaders were forced to escape to India.

What had happened in Black July 1983 was not an ethnic riot in the course of which Sinhala masses spontaneously attacked Tamil minorities. It was an organised attack by the ruling elite. To this day no investigation into the events has been carried out nor compensation paid to the victims.

The 1983 killings are considered a turning point in Sri Lankan history. The pogroms of that year had the effect of ensuring that Tamil armed struggle would get the support it needed from the Tamil masses. Youth from all over the country either joined existing militant groups or formed new ones. It is believed that over 35 organisations were formed in the 1980s. Significantly, the JVP was able to recruit young people, including Tamil youth from the plantations.

However, by this time there were already a number of other Tamil militant organisations and units in existence. One such was the People's Liberation Organisation of Tamil Eelam (PLOTE) which had been set up in 1979 by Uma Maheswaren. Maheswaren had been expelled from the LTTE for, allegedly, having a relationship with female member of the party – the LTTE forbade its members to intermarry or enter into relationships with other members.

With thousands of youth in the north and east joining PLOTE, it quickly grew into a large organisation. Its programme also had socialism as an objective and all the cadres went through classes of 'political education' although these classes did not always provide an accurate understanding of socialism.

An organisation responsible for recruiting and politically educating students for the movements' militant armed groups, was the Eelam Revolutionary Organisation of Students (EROS). EROS was committed to Marxism. It also had strong links with students in the United Kingdom and in other countries. These students helped EROS to form connections with the PLO and other revolutionary organisations throughout the world.

One organisation, the Tamil Eelam Liberation Organisation (TELO) was formed by ex-members of the LTTE and EROS. With support from the Indian state intelligence agency RAW, TELO grew rapidly. It claimed to have more weapons than any other group.

The Eelam People Revolutionary Liberation Front (EPRLF) was another militant group that originated in 1980 from student groups. Initially, its leading members had argued that, before forming a militant armed wing, they needed to mobilise the masses. Initially, EPRLF was the only group that was open to socialist ideas but, after 1983, it came into competition with rapidly expanding groups such as PLOTE and, in the end, its existence was brought to an end by the LTTE.

All the militant groups adopted the Vaddukoddai Resolution and promised to fight for a socialist revolution. Almost all of them distanced themselves from TULF. However a number of their leaders maintained close relationships with the TULF leader, A Amirthalingam, who was responsible for popularising separatism within TULF.

The LTTE leader, Prabhakaran, influenced by Amirthalingam, succeeded in making a breakthrough into the Dravidian parties in Tamil Nadu. He secured considerable amounts of funding from these parties. Chief Minister and ADMK leader, MG Ramachandran, publicly donated ten million Indian Rupees, a very large sum at that time, to the LTTE. His support, added to the LTTE's reputation as a disciplined group, led to significant gains for the LTTE.

In 1983, when it attacked a military truck, the LTTE had only just over 30 full-time members but, within a year, their recruitment and funding began to grow fast.

Despite calling themselves socialist revolutionaries, almost all the groups relied on funding from Indian Intelligence or Dravidian parties and businessmen from Tamil Nadu. The EPRLF sought various radical ways of fundraising. Its members kidnapped an American couple and demanded ransom, but their action was condemned by other militants as well as by the masses. Methods such as these were soon abandoned as counterproductive.

Meanwhile tension between the militant groups was increasing. In 1984, as antagonism between leaders intensified, an attempt in India to bring them together under one roof, failed. As murders and brutalities in the training camps increased, paranoia about security also intensified. The term 'traitor to the cause' came into common usage. The leaders went underground and travelled with bodyguards. The scene was set for a showdown between the groups.

At the same time as Indian government influence among the militant groups grew, the US and other western governments began to exercise greater influence in Sri Lanka. JR Jayewardene's decision to welcome western investment and the involvement of western imperialism, including the possibility of a US military base in Trincomalee, angered the Indian establishment. When the 'Voice of America' radio station began operating from Trincomalee, the Indian government saw it as direct provocation.

The Indian government took the decision to use the northern youths' struggle to teach the south a lesson and establish control over the entire island. Various armed groups were permitted to open training camps in Indian territory. They were given large sums of money and weapons and, in some cases, Indian military training.

Indian support changed both the character of the militant Tamil groups and conditions in the north and east of Sri Lanka. In the two years after Black July of 1983, all the movements had grown stronger and were able to hold back the Sri Lankan army from Jaffna port and Palali airport as well from other strategic strongholds. They also led a number of successful retaliatory strikes. The possibility of taking control by force of government-held territory in the north and parts of the east became real. With India supplying arms, some of the groups grew fast and, it must be said, became increasingly competitive. Personal rivalries and rivalries among groups about territorial control became a major problem. These disputes began to involve the use of weapons and the 'liberation movements' turned into killing machines. The internal killings that took place in 1985 and 1986 claimed up to 1,000 young lives. All attempts at uniting the armed groups failed.

To a major extent, as Indian influence began to dominate TELO, ideology and political motivation were side-lined. All the groups claimed they were fighting for a separate Eelam but none of them would seem to have had a clear political perspective. Most claimed to be following 'Marxist' methods but, with no true political perspective, were forced to prioritise the armed operation.

TELO's close cooperation with the Indian secret service angered the groups. However it was the LTTE that took full control. In one night in 1986, the LTTE attacked all the camps of TELO and the other groups. What followed was a brutal battle between armed groups. It was a major bloodbath and the means by which the LTTE established itself as the one and only Tamil armed group.

Indian involvement

Members from other groups splintered. Many left for Europe in fear of their life. Some sought protection from the Indian government and began to work for them. Some joined the Sri Lankan government with the sole aim of revenging the LTTE. This led to the formation of paramilitary organisations which worked with the Sri Lankan military and the Sri Lankan secret service.

Those who left maintained a deep hatred for the LTTE leadership. Their sole aim, opposing the LTTE, blinded them to the needs of the struggle for rights of the Tamil people and has led them down a path of very mistaken politics, including the justification of the Sri Lankan government's slaughter of Tamils. This remains a problem today.

Meanwhile JR Jayewardene's implementation of neoliberal policies was in full swing. The Reagan-Thatcher period of the 1980s marked the rise of neoliberalism worldwide. In order to maintain and forward their interests, imperialist powers supported dictatorships and brutal governments around the world.

Even after the 1983 pogroms, JR Jayewardene had no problem in securing support for his regime from the US and other western countries. Israel, with the US Embassy, operated a special interest section which helped in the training and arming of the Sri Lankan military. Pakistan, under US influence, also helped to arm and train the Sri Lankan military. In 1985, JR Jayewardene made a state visit to Pakistan.

During the Korean and the Indo-China wars, Trincomalee Harbour on Sri Lanka's north east coast, gained strategic importance. India and all the regional powers had an interest in this harbour. There was even talk of giving partial control of the harbour to the US military. Angered by this talk, the Indian government defined the proposal as coming from a 'Washington-Islamabad-Beijing axis' working against India. Rajiv Gandhi, leader of the Congress party and, later, prime minister, was said to have become impatient with the LTTE's domination in the north and JR Jayewardene's policies in the south. Jayewardene, who, during Mrs Gandhi's reign, had ignored Indian support for the militants, began to take security precautions against India.

The LTTE, having established its domination, moved to take control of the territories in the north. It justified its actions against the militants on the grounds that these actions led to a fall in criminal activity. Upper-class Tamils in the north partly saw the LTTE's action as something that 'had to be done' to win a separate

Tamil Eelam and continued to support the LTTE. With that support it was not difficult for the LTTE to gain control of rural territories. Some of these territories did not have government offices let alone police stations. Even in Jaffna, the opportunist Tamil upper class, partly in fear, supported the LTTE. However, the majority of recruits to the LTTE initially came from the region called Vadamarachchi, Prabhakaran's birth place.

To further its interests in Sri Lanka, the Indian government was keen to maintain its influence among the militants and gain regional domination. But India's interests conflicted with those of Western imperialists. With the blessing of the Western imperialists, the Sri Lankan government decided to take military action to re-capture land in the north from the LTTE. The government took this decision knowing full well that it would involve major loss of life. The first military operation began on 26 May 1987. The operation was named 'Operation Liberation' but was better known as the 'Vadamarachchi operation'.

Under the command of Brigadier Denzil Kobbekaduwa, approximately 10,000 troops marched to Vadamarachchi to capture the LTTE leader and the territory the LTTE controlled. Major Gotabaya Rajapaksa, currently defence minister in the government of his brother Mahinda Rajapaksa, led one of the battalions. A battle broke out which reportedly cost thousands of lives. Over 10,000 people, including 700 soldiers and a similar number of LTTE cadres, are said to have been killed.

By the beginning of June the army had come close to taking full control of north. Even though the LTTE had grown and was fully armed it was unable to repulse the massive military force which brutally shelled and bombed everything in its path.

During the operation, a mass protest was mounted by the Tamil Nadu people. Supported by Dravidian parties, Tamil Nadu condemned the military operation. Fishermen bringing food and supplies to the north were intercepted and prevented from entering the area by the Sri Lankan navy. It was at this time, when it seemed that the LTTE defeat was inevitable, that the Indian Air Force entered Sri Lankan air space. It did so illegally.

On 4 June Indian Transport Aircraft escorted by Mirage 2000 fighter planes dropped about 25 tonnes of food. The sound of the Mirage 2000 was different from the sounds the people had heard before. Rumours spread among the people and so did hope.

India's provocative action took the Sri Lankan government

by surprise. The Delhi authorities justified Operation Poomalai (Operation Garland, as it came to be known), as: "in keeping with its [India's] commitment to provide humanitarian assistance to the long-suffering and beleaguered people of Jaffna, the government of India was despatching consignments of urgently-needed relief supplies by air which would be para-dropped over Jaffna by transport aircraft. These IAF transport aircraft would be duly escorted to ensure their defence in case they are attacked while in flight."

Cowed by this action, the Jayewardene government called off Operation Liberation. On 29 July 1987 negotiations between the Sri Lankan and Indian governments were concluded. After Rajiv Gandhi signed the pact, he was attacked by a naval rating during a guard of honour. Rajiv ducked and narrowly escaped. The next day, the first Indian Infantry Brigade to arrive, calling itself the Indian Peace Keeping Force (IPKF), landed in northern Sri Lanka. There was euphoria among the Tamils masses who garlanded the soldiers in welcome.

The 13th amendment

By passing the 13th amendment to the constitution in August 1987, the government claimed that it devolved power to the Tamils in the country. The Sri Lankan parliament passed the amendment in November 1987. According to this amendment to the 1978 constitution, nine provinces were established (north, east, north central, north western, Sabaragamuwa, Uva, central, southern, western). Each province would have a governor appointed by the president who maintained almost all the powers including finance and security. Many military commanders occupied these posts. A chief minister was to be elected to all provinces but with no real powers. In effect the provinces gave a false impression of devolution of power, though almost every administrative function came under the executive power of the president and his appointed governor.

Though initially the north and east were separate provinces these were united into one province in September 1988 by the president according to the Indo-Lanka accord. No vote was held in the east for the agreement of this union; it was done under the power given to the president. This north and east provinces' merger took place mainly to control these territories under one 'security' operation.

Annamalai Varatharajah Perumal, previously a key leader of the

EPRLF, became the first chief minister of the merged province in the election held in November 1988. The EPRLF was operating as a paramilitary wing of the Indian military at that time. The Tamil National Army created through forced recruitment by the Indian military and the EPRLF was employed to force people to vote. The horror they unleashed still haunts many who lived in that period. It was a largely rigged election and in no means conducted democratically. Varatharajah Perumal was simply seen as toy of the Indian authorities.

When the IPKF was forced to leave in March 1990 Varatharajah Perumal and the rest of the EPRLF went with them. But just before he left Perumal pulled a stunt and moved a motion declaring 'Independent Eelam'! The newly elected President Ranasinghe Premadasa swiftly used his executive power to dissolve the provincial council. This was held under direct control of the president until 2008 when an election was held in the east after the 'de-merger'. The northern and eastern provinces were de-merged on 1 January 2007 after a JVP-led petition at the supreme court was upheld by the court in October 2006. The JVP used this and many other ways to sabotage the peace process that started in 2002. It was only the USP that fought back against this case. The argument that the court does not have a say according to the Indo-Lanka Accord or according to the 13th amendment was ignored – obviously for political reasons. Paramilitary forces once again triumphed in the eastern province election.

Opposition to Indian involvement

The LTTE, initially welcomed the Indian government's decision to enter the conflict. However, when the Indian government brought back members of the militant groups and sought to force the LTTE to agree a peace accord, the LTTE began to step back.

In the south, the ruling class was split. A faction within the UNP, under R Premadasa, opposed the Indian Army's presence in Sri Lanka. The SLFP announced that, were it in power, it would not have made as many concessions as Jayewardene made.

The JVP, having re-grouped as a small force with a strong communal leaning, vehemently opposed the pact. New recruits were versed in the concept of Indian expansionism. The presence of the Indian Army in Sri Lanka helped the JVP to recruit in the universities. The party began to grow again.

Whipping up Sinhala nationalism was made easy due to Indian military presence – which played into the fear of foreign occupation and loss of identity among ordinary Sinhalese people. Although the Indian authorities made assurances that they posed no threat to Sri Lankan sovereignty, this did not stop the JVP spreading rumours about division of the country.

As part of their vigorous campaign they carried out numerous killings and attacks. They attempted to shut down a number of government offices, etc. But the UNP government reacted brutally, unleashing its force to suppress the JVP. It is estimated that over 7,000 Sinhala youth were murdered by the government. Thousands were imprisoned. Many left the country in fear. In November 1989 the JVP leader Rohana Wijeweera was shot dead. The JVP never properly recovered from this brutal suppression. It also became more nationalist in its character, which later led it to join the SLFP government and to support the war that killed hundreds of thousands.

For the Indian ruling classes, Indian intervention had proved popular. Not only had India's actions rallied the support of the Tamil Nadu masses but they had also established Tamil ascendancy in the region. Before it intervened, the Congress party of Rajiv Gandhi had lost control in all the southern states. To make matters worse for Congress, several of its leaders faced corruption charges. Rajiv was able to turn this unpopularity around for a period with the intervention which the Indian nationalist ruling elite also thought would benefit India. Rajiv's administration had already moved closer to western imperialism than any previous Congress administration had.

Consolidating the control of the capitalist class by signing a new agreement and disarming the militants was in the interest of the Indian, Western and Sri Lankan ruling classes. JR Jayewardene was given full backing by Western governments. Thatcher praised his 'persistence and courage'. US President Ronald Reagan expressed his growing admiration for JR Jayewardene's wise leadership. He told Jayewardene that "the agreement... represents a vital step in the process of restoring island-wide peace and the tranquillity necessary for you and your government to concentrate on the economic and social equation". However, opposing India would mean a war with India – which none of the western countries was prepared to risk. As everyone benefitted greatly from the agreement, there was no economic basis for such a war.

In Sri Lanka, almost all the militant groups were under the control of RAW and approved the accord. But to the LTTE, the agreement constituted a threat. Having already lost a number of cadres in the war, the LTTE faced losing out to the other groups. For a long time, it had maintained that its ultimate aim was the creation of a separate state. But the first line of the so-called peace agreement read: "Desiring to preserve the unity, sovereignty and territorial integrity of Sri Lanka..." In fact, apart from generalities about preserving a multicultural society, etc, the agreement consisted of only one major point: namely, the proposal for a merger of the north and east into one unit. Sub-headings listed the criteria for the implementation of the proposal. To meet Jayewardene's request, a referendum would be held. The idea was that the Tamil areas would form a unit to be administrated by Tamils with semi-autonomic rights. However, the agreement did not specify how the administration would be constituted nor what amendments to the constitution would be made.

An appendix to the agreement required that "Tamil militants surrender their arms to the authorities". It also stated that "an Indian peacekeeping contingent may be invited by the president of Sri Lanka to guarantee and enforce the cessation of hostilities, if so required". The agreement included the letters of communication between JR Jayewardene and Rajiv Gandhi. In one of the letters JR Jayewardene agreed that:

"Trincomalee or any other ports in Sri Lanka will not be made available for military use by any country in a manner prejudicial to India's interests.

"The work of restoring and operating the Trincomalee oil tank farm will be undertaken as a joint venture between India and Sri Lanka. Sri Lanka's agreements with foreign broadcasting organisations will be reviewed to ensure that any facilities set up by them in Sri Lanka are used solely as public broadcasting facilities and not for any military or intelligence purposes. In the same spirit India will:

"Deport all Sri Lankan citizens who are found to be engaging in terrorist activities or advocating separatism or secessionism;

"Provide training facilities and military supplies for Sri Lankan forces, and;

"India and Sri Lanka have agreed to set up a joint consultative mechanism to continuously review matters of common concern in the light of the objectives stated in Para 1 and specifically to monitor the implementation of other matters contained in this letter."

The 'foreign broadcasting organisation' mentioned in one of the letters obviously referred to the 'Voice of America's operation in Sri Lanka. This reference was the key part of the agreement. It meant that India would control the Tamil militants and, in return, Sri Lanka would safeguard India's interest in Trincomalee and its economic interest in Sri Lanka as a whole. The agreement was a victory for the Indian and Sri Lankan ruling classes.

The LTTE, despite understanding at least in part the motives of the Indian and Sri Lankan governments, was, for several reasons, unable to oppose the agreement. First, it had lost support for continuing the arms struggle. Having suffered a great deal during the war, its supporters were relieved by the very suggestion of a peace agreement – regardless of its content. The LTTE also came under massive pressure from the Indian government. On 24 July the LTTE leader, Prabhakaran was flown to India in a military helicopter for negotiations with Rajiv Gandhi. In India, he found himself under house-arrest and forced to sign the agreement. To obtain his release, the LTTE members organised protests in Jaffna. He was finally released on 2 August after agreeing to surrender all arms.

Unable to win public support for the continuation of the war, Prabhakaran, at a mass meeting held in a northern town Suthumalai, announced that he would surrender arms. This meeting was the first mass meeting organised by the LTTE and the first public meeting at which Prabhakaran spoke. More than 100,000 people attended to learn their fate.

Ten years previously, Prabhakaran, as a young man, had been snubbed by the TULF. Now he was a commanding authority among the people. In his speech he gave an account of his negotiations with Rajiv Gandhi. He said: "this agreement is made without consulting Tamil people and implemented with urgency... (it) did not concern the problems of Tamils... (it) is primarily concerned with the Indo-Sri Lankan relations".

He concluded: "My beloved people, we have no way other than cooperation with this Indian endeavour. Let us offer them this opportunity. However, I do not think as a result of this agreement there will be a permanent solution to the problems of the Tamils. The time is not very far off when the monster of Sinhala racism will devour this agreement."

Although the masses wanted peace he was loudly applauded when he announced that the LTTE would surrender its weapons to the IPKF. He insisted, however, that, instead of armed struggle, the LTTE would continue the fight 'politically.' But the LTTE failed to work out how the 'political fight' would be conducted. Reluctance to enter into armed struggle was reinforced when a number of militants returned with IPKF protection to open new offices in the north and east. Many of the LTTE cadres, including their leaders, feared revenge attacks.

The LTTE demanded of the IPKF and the Indian authorities that it be the sole representatives in the new administration. Within weeks, assassinations of militants by other militants began. The LTTE used the situation as an opportunity to discredit the presence of the IPKF. It began an aggressive campaign using a variety of tactics against the presence of IPKF in the north.

One of the Tigers' most successful campaigns in rebuilding mass support was a hunger strike by the LTTE political leader Amirthalingam Thileepan. On 15 September 1987 he began his fast with five demands. They included the stopping of the Sinhala colonisation, withdrawal of the Sri Lankan military and the release of political prisoners. He also called for a referendum and the immediate formation of an interim administrative council.

In the eyes of the masses these were reasonable demands to which the IPKF appeared to have already agreed. But, in practical terms, none of the demands could be fulfilled within the time-frame proposed. On a prominent stage in Nallur in Jaffna town, Thileepan's highly publicised fast went ahead. Thousands queued to meet him and give him their support. A good orator, Thileepan continued to deliver speeches until, due to his weakening condition, he lost his voice.

As the days passed mass tension increased. On 26 September Thileepan was medically examined and, after checking his breathing and pulse the doctor put his head at Thileepan's feet and wept. The hundreds of people queuing to pay their respect to Thileepan were also engulfed in emotion. The scene was broadcast live on television and the people were immersed in sadness. In many houses, in respect for Thileepan, no meals were prepared. To win the approbation of the people, the LTTE, in spite of being given guarantees that their demands would be met, continued to support Thileepan in his fast. Death was inevitable. From Prabhakaran's 4 August speech until Thileepan's death on the 26 September, the LTTE gained a great deal of public support in its fight against the IPKF. But, reportedly, the LTTE continued its attack on the Sinhala people in the east.

On 2 October 1987, the Sri Lankan authorities arrested most of the leaders, and a number of members of the LTTE – 17 in all. Among the leaders were Pulenthiran and Kumarappa. They were held at the Palali northern air base while awaiting transfer to Colombo. On 5 October, the day they were to be transferred, all 17 swallowed cyanide, dying instantly. Fearing the LTTE retaliation the IPKF arrested a number of its members. The IPKF also raided the LTTE media premises and arrested several journalists. JR Jayewardene banned the LTTE and within a week there was an exchange of fire between the LTTE and the IPFK. A bounty of one million rupees was placed on Prabhakaran's head.

The exchange of fire between the LTTE and the IPKF developed into a brutal war. Fighting continued until 25 October. Both sides suffered heavy losses. A conservative estimate puts the number of causalities at over 1,000 people while over two million people were displaced. Both the LTTE and IPKF suffered heavy loss of life.

The suffering caused by the IPKF made the Indian military intervention extremely unpopular. The massacres that took place, the random arrests and the detention of young people, particularly the imprisonment, rape and other sexual assaults against women, made sure that the IPKF was bitterly hated by the masses.

Mounting opposition to the IPKF presence was even expressed within the UNP by Ranasinghe Premadasa. When he was elected in the presidential election held in January 1989, he began his campaign to get the Indian forces out of Sri Lanka. The LTTE began to cooperate with Premadasa to resist the Indian military, at times using Sri Lankan military equipment and vehicles.

This created an enormous embarrassment for the Indian government. Following the failure of Rajiv Gandhi in the election in December 1989 Indian policy in relation to the IPKF changed immediately. Due to enormous pressure in the country the newly-elected VP Singh ordered the troops to pull back.

Following the withdrawal of the Indian military, war between the LTTE and the government started quickly. Rajiv Gandhi was later assassinated on 21 May 1991 and Premadasa was assassinated on 1 May 1993. Both assassinations were believed to have been done by the LTTE.

Missed opportunity

Promise of peace during this period created enormous expectations among the working masses. They believed they could return to normal life while having made advances towards securing some of their rights. If the peace could be maintained and serious concessions were made, there could have been a retreat of nationalism in all communities.

Demand for a separate Tamil Eelam without building support in the south and in India remained a utopian dream. The 'minority' population could not win a military battle in the long-run against the Sinhala state, though it could prolong it due to its relative strength and other factors.

We saw, however, the logical conclusion of the military campaign later in the history. When the guns and logistics support of the imperialist powers joined force, Mahinda Rajapaksa was able to carry through a genocidal slaughter to establish complete military domination. This was also aided by the cover provided by George W Bush's 'War on Terror' idea in the aftermath of 9/11 which undermined support for the LTTE.

Even during the IPKF period, when Indian state involvement revealed the nature of the Sri Lankan state, the imperial interests including India's, the bloody endgame could have been predicted.

Sadly no strong political force existed on the ground that could articulate such an understanding and put forward a strategy to avoid it and fight for the rights of Tamils with clarity. With the exception of some, such as some of the members of Committee for a Workers' International, the left has tended to shift in whatever direction the wind blew.

The LTTE struggled for its survival as it was side-lined from the so-called peace process and faced a threat of being overwhelmed by the Indian military. While the LTTE was pushed into a corner and forced to defend its very existence, the rest of the militants operating under the wing of the Indian military created fear in the community in the name of Tamil nationalism. This further discredited the so-called peace efforts.

JVP on the other hand used all its strength to use this opportunity to spearhead fear mongering among the Sinhala working masses. They dressed up horrendous chauvinism in Marxist phraseology. They argued in the name of anti-imperialism – ie Indian expansionism – all masses should unite to preserve Sri Lanka's sovereignty. To this end they were even prepared to work with and defend part of the Sri Lankan capitalist class. For different reasons – ie in the name of defending themselves – the LTTE also drew a similar conclusion to work with the Sri Lankan government. Out of this triumphed the traditional capitalist force, the UNP, a key player under JR Jayewardene in stoking the fires of war. However the ruling elite were also partially divided at that time. Their weakness was exposed by the Indian military invasion.

A further and crucial factor existed – with regards to a force that could put forward a clear perspective for the successful struggle for the masses, a political vacuum existed. Needed was a force that could challenge India's regional ambition, while not creating any illusions in the Sri Lankan state. It must also be able to deliver serious concessions for the Tamils, at least partially meeting their national aspirations, and at the same time addressing the real concerns of the Sinhala working masses while also confronting the emerging nationalism and those groups trying to thrive on it.

Arguably only one force that existed in the country had the political potential to take up this mammoth task – the NSSP. The NSSP continued to command support among a layer of the Sinhala working masses and at the same time enjoyed enormous respect among the Tamil masses. Some of its leaders were household names in the Tamil areas at that time.

Unfortunately a key leader of the NSSP at the time, Vickramabahu Karunaratne, argued in support of Indian imperialism. He took a view that was directly opposite to that of the JVP and equally formulaic. He and some his supporters at the time had been taken in by the initial support among Tamils in response to the arrival of the IPKF. Instead of clearly explaining the character and intentions of the pro-capitalist Indian state, they colluded with the illusion that this intervention may bring forth some sort of 'solution' for the Tamil masses. These fundamental errors of superficial understanding and short-termism became a trademark of the NSSP that still persists.

It must not be interpreted that pointing to the failure of the left is any endorsement for the politics of the right wing or the government. This book first and foremost illustrates how the politics of the right and their class interests presented grave perils to the interests of the oppressed and working masses as a whole.

Some Tamil right-wing forces, while seeking opportunities to advance their economic standing through deals with the Sinhala nationalist state, often try to discredit the left. Incredibly some of them even claim that the left was responsible for "all the problems". Nothing could be further from the truth. These people are only loyal to their own class interests – ie their own profit interest – which most of the time precedes any other interests. They viciously twist, turn and bend history for their short-term profit gains. Right-wing parties are generally more divided and naturally lean towards policies that only serve a tiny wealthy elite.

Acknowledging the mistakes of some on the left, however, is vital to avoid making such errors in the future.

Failure of the left

The LTTE banned all political parties in the north and east. The ban had a major impact on the left as a whole and on trade unions in particular. Gradually all trade union activity came to a halt. Political discussion and debate ceased. There was no clear leadership of the left. The NSSP and its key leader Vickramabahu Karunaratne, was unable to fill the vacuum. What analysis of the situation existed at the time was erratic and non-Marxist.

On 25 November, a document prepared by Vickramabahu was distributed. The document was entitled 'Letter to Tamil Sama

LSSP office in Colombo, Left Federation platform on the road to opposition, May Day 1987

Samajits'. In it he declared: "There is no question that Prabhakaran is a terrorist", adding: "as far as I can see Uma [PLOTE leader] is not advocating terrorism". But by 1987 he had switched sides and become a supporter of Indian imperialism on the grounds that the Indian government purported to oppose US and other western imperialism.

Marxist followers in the NSSP formed themselves into a left group. Siritunga Jayasuriya was a key leader of the group. The following is an extract from Siritunga's book on the collapse of the NSSP: 'The Left: Discourse and Reality and Expectations':

On the collapse of NSSP:

> *"Theoretical discourse began to unwind between the Majority Group and the Minority Group of the NSSP, which we believe has much relevance to today's timely and on-going dialogue for a reawakening of the Leftist movement. The label of 'majority' or 'minority' was according to the votes each group received at the 1986 NSSP party Congress. The Majority Group was led by Vickramabahu, Vasudeva, Linus, Neil Wijethilaka and others, while the Minority Group was given leadership by Siritunga Jayasuriya, KW Jayathilaka…"*

> *"By 1988, debates within the NSSP on international developments and theoretical and political issues had become heated. The majority in the party decided that the debates should be discontinued and that burning issues, such as the Indo-Lanka Accord of 1987, be swept under the carpet. Many NSSP members were not sure whether certain people in the Minority Group were, in fact, NSSP members.*

> *"The NSSP deviated from the Marxist method of dialectical analysis and, instead of analysing the class character and perspectives of the Sri Lanka Mahajana Pakshaya (Sri Lanka People's party) of Vijaya Kumaranatunga, it concluded, wrongly, that the Mahajana party was a workers' party, and at that, the leading workers' party in the country. This deviation was not simply mistaken: it signified the Majority Group's capitulation to the petty-bourgeois so-called radicals who, in turn, were mesmerised by the film-idol image of Vijaya Kumaratunga. The Minority Group struggled against this deviation. In response, the Majority Group verbally attacked the Minority Group – sometimes physically. In effect, in order to make the NSSP attractive to the petty*

bourgeoisie, the Majority Group's leaders betrayed the party leading its members down a blind alley and it did so at a time when what was needed was support for the anti-UNP struggle.

"The Peoples' Liberation Front (JVP), then a banned party, was struggling against the UNP rule of JR Jayewardene and of 'Indian hegemony'. At this point, the JVP set out to kill the candidates for the provincial elections who supported the Indo-Lanka Pact. Vijaya Kumaratunga, LW Panditha, Upali Vithanage, DMD Chandrawimala, Douglas Kaluarachchi, Wimalasena of the government press and many other Sama Samaja, Communist, NSSP and Mahajana party activists were killed by the Deshapremi Janatha Vyaapaaraya (DJV, Patriotic Peoples' Movement), a movement attached to the JVP. Instead of opposing the assassinations and racism in general, the old Left leaders and, even, the NSSP Majority Group leaders, in order to obtain guns and ensure their own survival, muted their opposition to the government of JR. When the Minority Group demanded that the murderous racist insurgency of the petty-bourgeoisie be confronted and destroyed, their voice was stifled by the NSSP leadership. The leaders of the Majority Group branded the Minority Group trouble-makers and 'crypto-JVPers', and succeeded in having the entire Minority Group expelled from the party.

1987 May Day led by the Vama tendancy

"The history of the NSSP, since the day the minority was expelled, vindicates the minority's ideology and perspectives. Sinhala racism at its vilest, the flaunting of the capitalist parties' extreme reactionary politics, the government's campaign of murder of Tamil people and of repression of their media, all are consequences of the marginalisation and impotence of the Left movement of today. With the party's internal democracy strangled by the Majority Group's leadership's, the Minority Group was bereft of its party, the party its members had loved more than their own lives; the party which its members had built with blood, sweat and tears. To face the challenges that they knew were to come, they formed the Marxist Workers' Tendency, the pioneering organisation which today bears the name, the United Socialist party (USP).

"The stance of the NSSP was that even the Red Army had no right to enter a country albeit for the sake of revolution – a pacifist stance. Yet, in 1987, the NSSP supported the Indo-Lanka Pact – a pact that was a murderous conspiracy of two capitalist regimes and which was aimed at the throats of the Tamil workers, the Sinhala workers, and the workers of India! For the NSSP, the Pact was a fatal mistake. Joining the Indian and Sri Lankan capitalist class to crush the Tamil-speaking people's liberation struggle shattered the backbone of the party."

Police halt an illegal NSSP demo from the LSSP office, 1 May 1987

The above description of the debate that took place at the time of the Indian military intervention provides vital lessons for the future. Anyone who claims to build an 'organisation for the oppressed' must seriously approach the need for developing a correct strategy, without which building a strong force on the basis of short-term gains will result in zero gains. We saw how the enormous authority of the LSSP perished due to their mistakes. Now the JVP faces a similar fate of being reduced to rubble. The strength of an organisation that aims to lead the struggling masses lies on its ability to develop correct perspectives and then work out clear strategies.

Aftermath

With the intensification of war from the 1990s onwards the conditions of the Tamil masses deteriorated. The LTTE was strengthened and able to create a de facto state. While developing as a 'conventional military' force the LTTE begun to lose what remained of its ability to be flexible and adapt to changes. As a rigid force a series of mistakes were made, the mass expulsion of Muslims from the north being the most brutal.

The indiscriminate terror of Al-Qaeda provided ample opportunity for imperialist governments to consolidate mass support behind the Sri Lankan regime of Mahinda Rajapaksa after the 2005 elections. Following the horrific 9/11 incident, under George W Bush's rhetoric of the 'war on terror', a hunt was unleashed not just against the so-called 'terrorist' groups, but also against all forces that could potentially develop any opposition to imperialist interests. The LTTE also faced severe setbacks. Many western governments began to proscribe the LTTE and curb its international operations.

Reacting to this, the LTTE showed signs of willingness to enter peace negotiations. It also managed to force the Sri Lankan government to the negotiating table through significant military victories. The peace negotiations that began in 2002 once again created enormous expectations. However, once again reactionary forces such as the JVP began to oppose this.

The genuine and dearly held hopes of the masses for peace began to fade when tension between the Sri Lankan government and the LTTE started to increase. The defection of a key LTTE commander, Vinayagamoorthy Muralitharan, alias Karuna, significantly weakened the LTTE. Karuna took a number of cadres from the east with him and eventually joined forces with the government.

The developing and changing geopolitical situation including the rise of Chinese control in the region and aspiration to gain influence in Sri Lanka further strengthened the Sri Lankan regime. What followed was the 2009 genocidal war that saw the slaughter of tens of thousands of Tamils. The LTTE leadership and many of its cadres were brutally massacred too. The remaining LTTE leaders finally announced the end of their military campaign and said they will now participate in political struggle against the Sri Lankan state.

However the threat and horrendous treatment of the Tamil-speaking people in the country by the Sinhala nationalist state continues. Never have such intense attacks on democratic rights been seen on the island.

The regime continues to strengthen its military domination across the country and is creating a military dominant state. In this so-called peace time the defence budget is the largest ever, while the public spending allocation for education is reduced to an all-time low. Every social improvement won by the working class during the great battles in the past is now under serious threat.

In order to maintain power the dictatorial regime of Rajapaksa continues to propagate divisions among all communities. The Tamil-speaking Muslim community is targeted by the most chauvinist section which is directly supported by the defence secretary, the president's brother Gotabaya.

Even in these enormously difficult times, in the aftermath of the slaughter, we can see signs of fighting back. Even in this period workers' struggles have defeated this government on a number of occasions. Students have shown their bravery in standing up to the brutal state. Refugees have defied continuous military torture. The landless have heroically forced the military out. The list goes on. Though these are minor victories and events they should inspire confidence to build the strong struggle now required. Where there is oppression, there will emerge a fightback. The struggle will continue.

Conclusion

Today the Tamil youth and working people once again face the huge task of building a real fighting force that will provide clear political leadership.

Although this short historical narrative ends in 1990, there are numerous historical lessons in the events that followed. A number of books that expose the horror unleashed by the Sri Lankan government in 2009 are now emerging. The Cage: The fight for Sri Lanka and the last days of the Tamil Tigers, written by Gordon Weiss, is an important read. Though this book is written in good spirit, there are some historical/political facts that need to be pointed out in addition. A critical reading of Still Counting the Dead by Frances Harrison is also valuable. Reviews of both of these books are available on the Tamil Solidarity website: www.tamilsolidarity.org

Included in the appendix is a Tamil Solidarity article written in January 2012, which includes some key points that we cannot miss while working out the way ahead for the future struggle of the Tamil-speaking people.

Appendix 1: What way Ahead for the Tamil-speaking people's struggle?

First published January 2012

1. New period of crisis and struggle

We are now in the midst of the worst crisis of capitalism in generations, a crisis which is currently shaping the world around us. To speak of capitalism is to refer to the profit-motivated economic system that dominates the world today.

To understand the origin of the crisis and the way in which it has developed, it is important to understand how 99% of the population – the working classes and the unemployed - view the world. Equally important, is an understanding of the character and perspective of the 1% who control the wealth of the world.

A well-known free market economist, Nouriel Roubini, one of the few who predicted the crisis, points out that the nub of the problem is in the way the capitalist system works. The constant shift of income from labour (the exploited) to the capitalists (the exploiters) is, he warns, the major cause and one that could bring the entire system down.

As is well known, the ruling elite continue to ignore the systemic faults that cause crises. In an attempt to find a 'quick fix', ie to minimise falls in profit and the loss of banks and big business, the pockets of ordinary working people are progressively squeezed. And it is the ordinary people who are asked to pay for a crisis which is not of their making. In the West, a new era of struggle is beginning, a struggle in which, in the developed countries, demonstrations, strikes and occupancies are increasingly taking place. Suppression or control of the struggle are the foremost concern of the ruling class. To protect its interests, the ruling class manipulates the government, the police, the military, the courts, the media and whatever else it controls, against the opposition.

In this struggle over an ever-shrinking cake, rivalry between countries will inevitably increase, aiding the rise in nationalism and protectionism. Hence the coming period is being characterised, even by right-wing analysts, as a period of 'fragmentation economically and politically'.

Analysts amongst the left who predicted the crisis, point out that 'temporary fixes' will not solve the problem, that the problem is one systemic crisis and is likely to be a prolonged. They conclude that the period we have entered is one of minimal growth – if not of no growth at all - and of depression and its concomitants: rising unemployment, lack of investment in public services etc. In turn, the depression is giving rise to social unrest and is strengthening the will to fight back against the system trying to maintain its rule.

Prestigious projects of the ruling elite in the west, such as the euro project, have been rocked by a storm with Greece at its epicentre. The European parliament, which promotes itself as a guardian of democracy, is now insisting on un-elected 'technocrats' taking control of the affairs of Italy. David Cameron, the British Prime Minister, arrogantly announced that he will end the human rights culture. And it is clear that the ruling class will try to remain in power by whatever means possible.

From the point of view of the oppressed masses in Sri Lanka, the mark the struggling people the world over will leave on our history is important. The revolutionary struggles against powerful dictators that is spreading across North Africa and the Middle East, demonstrates the potential power of mass movements and provides a much-needed boost in confidence to people the world over..

We have seen the occupations of Wall Street in the US and elsewhere and, in Britain, the largest coordinated strike in eighty-five years. The struggles of the masses in so many parts of the world will define the coming years. The oppressed Tamil-speaking people, by participating in the global movement, will find a way to strengthen their movement.

2. Crisis – Asian, South Asian impact

The premise that the two fastest growing economies in the world, China and India, can save the world economy is now being questioned. China already faces what has been described as the 'next subprime' – a reference to the mortgages which triggered the financial meltdown in the US in 2008. A Barclays Capital report is just one of many financial documents expressing concern about the slowing down of the economy and the 'decline in trust lending in shadow banking' which constitutes about 22% of all financing in China. 'Social and political tensions might be a bigger worry,' the report concludes.

The Indian ruling elite share these concerns. Manufacturing industry has already been hit and growth expectations have been downgraded. The market is largely regarded as 'unstable'. The Economic Times reports that 'India is grappling with high inflation' and yet the Indian wealth gap has narrowed. Instead, the wealth gap has been widened further. Under Congress's rule, India has created both more billionaires and more poor than, proportionately, has any other country. About 42% of India's population (over 455 million) live on or below $1.25 per day. Over 300 million live on less than 50p a day. India's per capita income is ranked 139th in the world and two-thirds of the world's poor live in India. A staggering total of 150 million live in slums.

Pakistan is another country in the region that is increasingly unstable and aid-dependent. As part of their endeavour to counter trade competition with China, the US and the West are strengthening their ties with India and encouraging Pakistan to strike a deal with India.

All countries in the Eastern region, including Sri Lanka, are involved in the new geo-politics now developing. To the North, India, in an attempt to minimise the influence of China in Pakistan, is putting pressure on Pakistan to reject Chinese offers of friendship. Equally important to India is control of the Tamil Nadu in the South. The discovery of huge uranium deposits in Tamil Nadu is an additional reason for the dramatic change in attitude of Western countries towards India's nuclear development. Further, as the world's largest arms importer, India provides a market for which the Western Imperialists are competing to exploit.

However, it is not easy for the Indian government to counter the Tamil national consciousness developing among the Tamil Nadu masses. The corruption scandal, originating in Tamil Nadu, further exposed the baseness of the political elite. Ever-rising food and fuel prices have created an increasingly tense situation for the Central government.

During the war in Sri Lanka, the political elite in Tamil Nadu, in cahoots with Congress, played a major, but concealed role in the slaughter of many Tamil speaking Sri Lankans. The concealment minimised the possibility of protests in Tamil Nadu. Now, that their role has been exposed, the Indian Government will have to be wary of any further display of nationalism

Another possible danger faced by the elite is that the potential for the struggle against economic deprivation might merge with nationalist feelings. Maintaining a close link with the Sri Lankan government will require that a tough approach be taken to any possible Tamil nationalist developments in Tamil Nadu.

In the meantime the Sri Lankan government has developed a

close economic relationship with China which has invested in major undertakings in the building of ports, etc. in Sri Lanka. Therefore, it would be foolish to expect the Indian or Chinese governments to take a stand against the Sri Lankan government. In fact it was the Chinese, Indian, Pakistani and Iranian governments which collaborated in aiding the Sri Lankan government's war against the Tamil-speaking people. These countries continue to play a key role in blocking action against the war crimes committed in Sri Lanka by the Rajapaksa regime. While Western imperialists attempt to curtail Chinese influence in the region, they have no way of succeeding without the Indian Government's support. No outside action against the Sri Lankan government can be taken without the blessing of India.

The Sri Lankan regime enjoys a close relationship with the Indian government which complicates the task of those who want to see the Sri Lankan government brought to book for its war crimes. Western interests in the region are likely to be expressed through Indian foreign policy which makes it unlikely that even those sympathetic to the Tamil people in Sri Lanka will express or act on their sympathies. Expecting any government to act solely in the interest of human rights leads to disappointment only.

Declining economic growth in the region could lead to China exercising greater control over the economy and attempting to strengthen its influences in countries such as in Sri Lanka. It is possible that, in consequence, China might intensify its support for the regimes of such countries, regardless of their poor human rights record and regardless of internal opposition or international disapprobation. Neither the Chinese nor the Indian government has an exemplary human rights record.

3. Sri Lanka – development and growth?

The so-called 'post war growth' in Sri Lanka, which bypassed working-class people, has, in the main, been halted by the global economic crisis. In order to maintain its grip on the whole country, the current regime is, perforce, increasing its defence expenditure. In its 2012 budget, over $2 billion was allocated to defence. Even during the height of the war, defence expenditure did not reach this level. Repayment of debt adds further stress to the economy.

To prevent the 'exchange rate from depreciating', an appeal was made to the International Monetary Fund (IMF). This was the first time the Island had made such an appeal. In May, 2009, a loan of $2.6

billion loan was granted. However, the IMF required that specified conditions be met and is still withholding the final payment until all its demands are met. These demands include increasing taxes, freezing wages and cutting social expenditure. But the regime faces massive opposition to such policies. Attempts to alter the pension scheme were defeated after tens of thousands of workers took action. The action led to violence in the course which a worker was killed. In fear of further violence, the government enforced a curfew for the day of the funeral.

Chinese and Indian investment has so far helped the economy avoid collapse. But the slowing down of their economies is likely to have an impact on the Sri Lankan economy. On the positive side, relative peace on the Island has resulted in relative economic growth. Relative peace has allowed for the reconstruction of the infrastructure (during the War, the infrastructure, together with the lives of thousands, was reduced to dust.) Tourism and other industries are growing. Small businesses are opening and basic utilities such as electricity, mobile phone networks, etc. are functioning. But although there is a sense that things are improving, the actual gains for the local people are minimal.

The Government, thus far, has no plans to invest in developing industries, building new schools, universities or hospitals and thus creating new jobs. Most of the plans the Government does have are dependent on investment from India and China – which would require a move towards privatisation. But the Island's history of struggle culminating in civil war suggests that it would be difficult for the Government to make this move. The Governments iron grip on power and suppression of democratic rights are likely to persist. People in the south have never experienced an attack on democratic rights such as the current one. The Rajapaksa family controls every aspect of government. The military, under the control of the President's brother, has taken responsibility for civic functions such as control of urban development etc.

The conditions in the north are comparable to Indian-occupied Kashmir. People are yet to recover from the shock of the War. For the present, they have accepted the rule of their oppressors. The Government, knowing that the unchallenged overarching authority it now has can last only for a limited period, is, nevertheless, taking all the steps it can to protect the status-quo.

More military camps have been opened and the existing ones strengthened. The Sri Lankan military with over 200,000 personnel, is, proportionate to the size of the population, extremely large. The Sinhala language is in use throughout the Island: in school books, on sign posts, etc. and, in many instances, without Tamil translation.

Internally displaced people, refugees and war victims have not been resettled or given adequate compensation. The new generation has had to accept poverty as the norm. But the situation cannot continue and will be challenged. Even with the huge military presence, the constant intimidation and propaganda, the state machine will not be able to contain anger much longer.

4. Political developments in Tamil areas

The North and East of Sri Lanka approximate open prison camps. In these regions there is no freedom of speech nor is there any possibility of the emergence of truly independent political forces. The regions are controlled by paramilitary leaders loyal to the Rajapaksa family. The Tamil National Alliance (TNA), initially established by the LTTE, is the only significant Tamil political party not directly linked to the government.

Despite the hostile political climate, the Tamil-speaking people in the regions voted overwhelmingly to support the TNA. The TNA leadership tends to take this support and the lack of any alternative for granted. In reality, votes for the TNA are not votes for its policy, but votes against the government for, in fact, TNA seems to be doing the exact opposite of what people want.

The Government treats the TNA and all Tamil political activists as 'dummies'. For their part, many of the TNA leaders are only interested in making 'easy' money out of the post-war developments. They also believe that it is possible to negotiate with the regime. What they would negotiate about is not clear. Thus far, they have not asked for anything other than what has been demanded by the civil societies in the South. They have not expressed any view on the economy nor on how the budget is allocated, etc. They watch while large sums are allocated to the military. What they ought to be doing is taking an uncompromising stand in defence of the oppressed Tamil-speaking people and making clear the purpose of their struggle. At the very least, they should initiate discussion on these issues.

Even more detrimental to their cause, leading members of the TNA have begun to spread the idea that in order to win even minimal concessions, the Tamil-speaking people must rely on the Indian State. They assist in hiding the role the Indian government played in the final phase of the war. Some even insist that the Tamil-speaking people in Tamil Nadu and the Diaspora do not understand the 'ground reality'. They spread the idea that if anyone defends the interests of the Tamil-speaking people or speaks out against the war crimes, the Tamil-speaking people in Sri Lanka will be punished. They also maintain that lobbying imperialist powers such as the United Kingdom will push the Sinhala masses further into the hands of Sinhala chauvinists.

It is right that no illusions about the imperialist powers should be created. (Like many dictators, Rajapaksa uses anti-imperialist rhetoric to rally support.) It is clear that the imperialists' interests in the region are in no way the same as those of the oppressed masses. An important task for Tamil activists is to oppose imperialist pressures as well as those of the national and regional powers. To do so effectively, it is crucial that the activists link up with the struggling masses in the region and around the world – it is the masses who are their natural allies.

Linking with natural allies does not mean entering an alliance opportunistically to advance personal interests. Based on an understanding of common interests, it means struggling for decent living conditions, democratic rights, national rights, etc – all interests diametrically opposed to those of the ruling class whose main concern is to increase the profits of its members by increasing their grip on power and devising exploitative measures.

It also means fighting to reduce support for the ruling elite such as that currently provided by the TNA and the Dravidian parties in Tamil Nadu, both willing to compromise the interests' to gain allies' in the ruling parties. At the same time, in order to strengthen our struggle, we must go beyond ethnic, caste, religious or any other division and link up with our allies and potential allies. We need to identify progressive forces in the South with which we could unite in fighting the oppressive forces and taking up common issues. Expressing solidarity and participating in struggle will provide a common platform.

Further, Tamil-speaking people should express solidarity and seek to work with all people in the South who are willing to fight for their rights and better working conditions. At this stage, most Sinhala workers may not understand or be prepared to accept the demand of the Tamil-speaking people for the right to self-determination. But the Tamil speaking people should participate in Sinhala workers' strikes and other struggles for, at least, two important reasons: first, attacks on Sinhala workers are attacks against all, and it will be the

Tamil-speaking people who, in the end, will bear the brunt of the

Furthermore it is through the language of struggle that Southern working people will come to understand the plight of the Tamil-speaking people in the North. In the end, it will be this kind of solidarity that will cut across chauvinist propaganda.

The Sinhala Government will try, as they have for the last seventy years, to counter alliances of any sort between Sinhala and Tamil speaking people by means of divisive propaganda and by blaming the Tamil-speaking population for all manner of hardships including driving down living standards. But, in the long run, experience will lead these workers to learn who it is who is really responsible for their deteriorating conditions. And they must know that, when they are ready to fight back, the oppressed Tamil-speaking people will be with them.

The demand for the right to self-determination of Tamil-speaking people is the response to national oppression by the chauvinist Sinhala governments which mobilised the Sinhala people's support while continuing to exploit them. The Sinhala masses, having sacrificed many democratic rights, have seen no significant improvements in their living conditions. Instead the entrenched dictatorship is threatening all that was won in past struggles, including free education, health care, etc. The Sinhala masses' support for the Tamil speaking people's right to self-determination is not a threat to their existence or rights. Rather, it could serve to unite them in the struggle of all the oppressed against the system that exploits both Tamil and Sinhala peoples.

The argument for the Tamil speaking people of Sri Lanka linking up with the people of Tamil Nadu is the same as that for linking up with Sinhala Sri Lankans. The masses in Tamil Nadu, in their struggle against their powerful Central Government, will not make much progress on their own. But, in alliance with the oppressed Kashmiris and with other tribal people, they would constitute a real threat to the Government.

In any event, the future does not augur well for the Indian sub-continent. A population imbalance looms. For the first time in recorded history, two hundred and thirty million people will be aged between fourteen and twenty-one years, ie moving into adulthood and the employment market. With the prospect of a slowdown in the economy, the threat of large scale unemployment and its consequences looms. In any event, with the opening of Indian's economy to neoliberal exploitation, there is already considerable antagonism among India's youth towards corporations and the super-rich. For the Indian youth, the only real alternative is to enter the struggle. With the current corruption scandals involving all the major parties, the struggle of the youth and the working class as a whole for a better life will intensify.

The Indian State is the main enemy of the Tamil Nadu people. These people's understanding of the State's oppressive role is better than those of Tamils in the Diaspora or in Sri Lanka. Hence the fight against Indian regional hegemony cannot succeed without engaging those within India who are struggling against it. Progress in Tamil Nadu will strengthen the will of the Tamil speaking people of Sri Lanka to fight back.

The task of forging an alliance between people of the island and the mainland is made considerably easier by their having a common language and common culture. However there is considerable misunderstanding between the two communities. What is needed is the initiation of more discussion – not only about present day politics and perspectives but also about history. Much disagreement and confusion stem from the lack of common understanding.

So the task before the Tamil speaking people and their supporters elsewhere is not the 'quick fix' but, rather, the prolonged slog of building a joint struggle. However, in the wider world there is much in their favour: increasing understanding of the failure of the capitalist system and the crises it is causing: the growing realisation of the class nature of the fight and the recognition of 'them and us' in society. All these trends assist the task.

Appendix 2: About Tamil Solidarity

Tamil Solidarity, formerly Stop the Slaughter of Tamils (SST), was set up in response to the terrible slaughter of thousands of Tamil people, the siege in Sri Lanka's north-eastern coastal strip, the lack of medical aid, nutrition, water and sanitation. Hundreds of thousands of people were caught in this trap. They are now being held in militarised villages – in reality, open prison camps.

The first meeting of SST was held in Chennai, Tamil Nadu, India, in early-March 2009, bringing together Sri Lankan and Indian Tamils, trade union organisers, journalists, as well as Sinhala activists who are totally opposed to the brutal sectarian politics of the Rajapaksa government. It was followed by a public meeting of 600 people at which a statement from Arundhati Roy, the Booker Prize winning Indian author, was read.

The call to spread the campaign around the world was put out and, on 21 March, the SST held its first meeting in Britain. An International Day of Action was organised to highlight the Indian government's military aid to Sri Lanka and its big-business exploitation of the Sri Lankan economy. There were protests at Indian embassies in Britain, Ireland, Sweden, Israel, India and many other countries. Since then, the campaign has organised several protests, meetings, debates at universities etc.

Around the world, the Tamil Diaspora reacted to the slaughter of Tamil-speaking people with a ferocious and courageous protest movement. From the start, Tamil Solidarity supported these protests and continues to do so. It aims to build support and solidarity in every community and trade union and in other areas.

At its Congress in 2012, the largest public sector union in Britain, UNISON, voted to affiliate itself with the Tamil Solidarity campaign. In addition Tamil Solidarity enjoys the support of numerous trade union branches and trade union activists.

Appendix 3: Tamil Solidarity Platform

The following platform of demands has been agreed by the campaign. Appropriate slogans can be drawn from it for campaigning in different countries.

Tamil Solidarity: For the rights of workers and all oppressed people in Sri Lanka

1. An independent war crimes investigation!

For a people's tribunal consisting of representatives accountable to working class and poor people from all communities, chosen by them and observed by international trade union and human rights organisations. Only such a body could be truly free of the influence of the Sri Lankan government and their international collaborators.

2. Withdraw the troops!

For an immediate end to military operations in Sri Lanka. Withdraw the army from all Tamil areas. Stop the disappearances.

3. No to detention camps!

For the immediate shutdown of militarised detention camps. For the provision of food, shelter and health facilities to Tamil people, administered under the control of their own elected and accountable representatives.

4. Stop Arming Sri Lankan regime!

For an immediate end to military support for Sri Lanka by western imperialism and by India, China, Pakistan, Israel, Iran, Japan and other countries. No to loans from the pro privitisation IMF and the World Bank. Support action such as workers' boycotts of arms shipments.

5. Democratic rights for all!

For the freedom of speech and the media, freedom of association and the right to free and fair elections, the right of all to vote without interference, freedom to stand in elections for parties which accept equal rights for all, regardless of nationality, religion, caste and sex. Support the work of bodies like the Civil Monitoring Committee investigating kidnappings, disappearances and extra-judicial murders.

6. Support independent trade unions!

For full trade union rights, free from intimidation and state interference. Support campaigns by independent trade unions on workers' rights, pay and conditions to organise all working-class people, regardless of ethnic, religious or other differences. Unity is strength.

7. Defend the right to self-determination!

Support a mass movement of Tamil workers and poor for the right to determine their own future. Full and equal rights of any minorities to be guaranteed in all areas.

Allow the right of self-determination to the Tamil-speaking people, up to and including secession, according to their wishes, while safeguarding the rights of all minorities.

In addition Tamil Solidarity has made a stand against a number of issues, including the military land-grab, the state-sponsored violence against Muslims and minorities, and the attacks on women including sexual violence.

Additional demands put forward by Tamil Solidarity in Tamil Nadu, India

1. Support the struggle of all oppressed nationalities

We support the struggle of the workers and oppressed in Kashmir, and of other national minorities in the region. For the right to self-determination of all oppressed nationalities. We demand the repeal of the draconian Armed Forces (Special Powers) Act (AFSPA) and the withdrawal of armed forces from Kashmir and the North East states. We also demand an immediate halt to Operation Green Hunt, which is run by forces linked to the Indian state, through which countless farmers and tribal people have been killed.

2. Better condition for Tamil refugees

Tamil refugees who fled the horrendous war are still forced to live in unbearable conditions. We demand that special measures are taken to improve their living standard and education, and other rights must be made available for them. We also demand a speeding up of the granting of naturalisation for those refugees who had been suffering in India for many years.

3. Remove private interests and corruption

We demand an immediate end to corruption. This would provide huge amounts of money for the improvement of the lives of millions.

All those business and politicians involved in corruption to be tried by a jury of elected representatives of the workers and poor masses. Money returned should be invested in public services.

All privatisation of public services should be stopped immediately and key industries, such as the telecom industry etc, to be nationalised.

4. End the caste grip

We demand an immediate end to all discrimination based on caste. Immediate investment and improving of towns and villages where working and poor people are pushed to live and segregated based on caste. No to segregation along caste lines. For decent housing and decent jobs for all. End to the state-aggravated caste riots and violence, and for a wider education programme to involve the masses to fight back for their rights.

5. End the onslaught on the environment. Land to the landless

For an immediate end to the multinationals such as Vedanta, POSCO which are wrecking the live of the most vulnerable people. We demand an immediate halt to the mining and other projects that are poisoning and destroying the land and water and other resources.

Fight for the rights of the landless peasants. End the control of the land in the hands of big business.

Contact Tamil Solidarity

- www.tamilsolidarity.org
- join@tamilsolidarity.org
- International coordinator: TU Senan:
senan@tamilsolidarity.org
(00 44) 7 90 80 50 217
- England and Wales national coordinators:
Manny Thain: mannythain@tamilsolidarity.org
Keerthikan: keerthikan@tamilsolidarity.org

Appendix 4: Glossary

ACTC – All Ceylon Tamil Congress

CCP – Ceylon Communist Party

CNC – Ceylon National Congress

Communist Party (Maoist) also called Ceylon Communist Party (Peking Wing)

CTB – Ceylon Transport Board

CWC – Ceylon Workers' Congress

CWI – Committee for a Workers' International

DMK – Dravida Munnetra Kazhagam

Eelath Thamilar Ilangar Iyakkam (Eelam Tamils Youth Movement) 1969 and before

EPRLF – Eelam People Revolutionary Liberation Front

EROS – Eelam Revolutionary Organisation of Students

FP – Federal Party or Ilankai Tamil Arasuk Kadchi (ITAK, Lanka Tamil State Party)

GCSU – General Clerical Services Union

INC – Indian National Congress

JSS – Jathika Sewaka Sangamaya

JVP – Janatha Vimukthi Peramuna (People's Liberation Front)

LSSP – Lanka Sama Samaja Party (Lanka Equal Society Party)

LTTE – Liberation Tigers of Tamil Eelam

MEP – Mahajana Ekseth Perumuna (People's United Front)

NSSP – Nava Sama Samaja Party

PLOTE – People's Liberation Organisation of Tamil Eelam

RAW – Research and Analysis Wing

SLFP – Sri Lankan Freedom Party

TELO – Tamil Eelam Liberation Organisation

TLO – Tamil Liberation Organisation

TMP – Tamil Manavar Peravai – Tamil Students League

TNA – Tamil National Alliance

TNT – Tamil New Tigers

TULF – Tamil United Liberation Front

TYL – Tamil Youth League (Tamil Elaingyar Peravai)

ULF – United Left Front

UNP – United National Party

USP – United Socialist Party

VKR – Vaddukoddai Resolution